IN-LAWS, OUTLAWS
&
OTHER THEORIES OF RELATIVITY

Other books by Lynne Alpern and Esther Blumenfeld

THE SMILE CONNECTION:
HOW TO USE HUMOR IN DEALING WITH PEOPLE

MAMA'S COOKING

OH, LORD, I SOUND JUST LIKE MAMA

IN-LAWS, OUTLAWS
&
OTHER THEORIES OF RELATIVITY

Lynne Alpern and Esther Blumenfeld

Illustrated by Cal Warlick

PEACHTREE PUBLISHERS, LTD.
Atlanta

Published by
Peachtree Publishers, Ltd.
494 Armour Circle, NE
Atlanta, Ga. 30324

Manufactured in the United States of America

10 9 8 7 6 5 4 3 2 1

Library of Congress Cataloging in Publication Data

Alpern, Lynne
In-Laws, outlaws & other theories of relativity / Lynne Alpern and Esther Blumenfeld ; illustrated by Cal Warlick.
p. cm.
ISBN 0-934601-94-1
1. Family--United States--Humor. 2. Interpersonal relations--United States--Humor. 3. American wit and humor. I. Blumenfeld, Esther. II. Title. III. Title: In-Laws, outlaws, and other theories of relativity.
PN6231.F3A67 1990

818' .540208035204--dc20 89-26523
CIP

Cover design and illustration by Cal Warlick
Design by Candace J. Magee

Dedication

A few rose petals, please, for some long-time friends: Adele, Dian, Ina, Linda, Lynn, Marsha, Nancy, Natalie, Jim, Mort, Sid, Simon, Bob, Bob, Bob and my Bob, who always make the good times better and the bad times bearable; and for all my in-laws: an unforgettable collection of memory-makers, and not an oddball in the bunch, except...ask another question.

Lynne

For my husband, Warren, who blessed me with his folks, Fannie and Chuck; for my son, Josh, who's the cream of the crop by acclimation; for my brother David, who conjured up Rudina, Samara and Ari; for my parents Karl and Ruth, and the rest of the family—the reliable ones, the renegades, and the raconteurs whose stories never cease to delight.

Esther

Acknowledgments

Thanks to our editor, Helen Weil, who wields a comma better than anyone we know, our illustrator, Cal Warlick, and his magic quill, and all the other supportive people at Peachtree Publishers....any of whom would make palatable in-laws.

Our deepest appreciation to Ann Jacob for the use of the Ann Jacob Gallery; to Peter Polites for permission to photograph his splendid sculptures, "Balancing Act" and "Adult/Child Podium," and to our creative photographer, Nancy Maxwell Goldberg, who made it all come together.

CONTENTS

INTRODUCTION

Shortly after OH, LORD, I SOUND JUST LIKE MAMA was published, we received a letter from Lucy, who wrote, "I want to tell you how much I enjoyed MAMA. I gave my mother a copy, and it was passed around from sister to sister, daughter to mother, and was met with such a lively reaction that I gave my mother-in-law a copy and stirred up that side of the family.

"It prompted a lot of reminiscences and brought back lots of memories. We're looking forward to your next book dealing with in-laws. I certainly wish someone *would* deal with mine!"

We hope Lucy's wish comes true when she reads IN-LAWS, OUTLAWS & OTHER THEORIES OF RELATIVITY filled with advice, anecdotes and wry observations we heard from men and women all over the United States. We wrote them with lots of laughter and a sprinkling of love, because as far as we know that's the best way to deal with anyone.

Few folks escape the in-law experience completely. A statistician with time on his hands claims that 93.8% of American men and 95.4% of American women have married at least once by the age of 54, bringing with them the requisite number of in-laws. If you include the additional people who never wed but have siblings who present them, unbidden, with brothers-in-law or sisters-in-law, you can even become an in-law through no fault of your own.

So unless you plan to marry an only child who happens to be an orphan, you are well advised to take a long, hard look at those inherited parents, sons, daughters, siblings, aunts, uncles, cousins, nieces, nephews and grandparents. Then inhale, laugh and accept the inevitable, as one dazed young bride did when she first met her new family and sighed, "So these are the genes in my family pool."

At first we were going to call the book, "Oh, Lord, I Think I Like My In-Laws," until Esther's mother-in-law, Fannie, remarked, "I think it's going to be a very small book." She was right. That idea quickly shrank to chapter size. And although we didn't want this book to turn into "In-laws and Outlaws—The Scourge Of The West," some stories were simply too delicious to omit. So for balance (and truth) as well as for laughs we include the chapter, "Things We Would Never Put In This Book."

Many of the names are changed to protect the innocent/guilty, but, with permission, some remain the same. You know who you are. However, when your in-laws ask, you can always say. . . .Who me?

Lynne asked her parents for stories about their own in-laws. While her father commented, "The problem is, I can't remember," her mother sighed, "The problem is, I can't forget."

As Albert Einstein's mother-in-law always said, "Albert, it's $E=MC^2$. Now put down those papers and talk to me."

E.B. and L.A.

IN-LAWS, OUTLAWS
&
OTHER THEORIES OF RELATIVITY

CHAPTER 1

OKAY, WHO THREW THE RICE PUDDING?

(Weddings)

A WEDDING IS ALWAYS A TIME OF JOY . . . for the bridal consultant, the caterer, and the florist. For the unsuspecting couple, however, the joyful memories often lie unkindled until the photo album arrives.

It's a wonder weddings ever take place at all. You know how hard it is to arrange a family reunion? Throw in another clan of complete strangers—with heightened expectations, jangled nerves, shrinking bank accounts, black sheep, bizarre traditions, territorial imperatives and competitive parenting, plus a young couple who mistakenly think this is *their* wedding to plan, and stand back for the fireworks. Who OK'd Elmo the family retriever as the ring bearer at the garden wedding? What happens when the bride can't decide which of her father's three ex-wives she wants as her matron of honor? Whom do you seat next to Uncle Martin the shoe fetishist?

A few facts are universal: 1) no matter how many invitations are allotted to the groom's family, it's never enough; 2) the logistics for transporting out-of-towners requires the training of a battalion commander; 3) only two names will overlap the bride and groom's guest lists.

If a wedding looms in your future, here are a few survival tips for. . .

THE BRIDE: Practice saying "Yes, Mom, that sounds great."

THE GROOM: Dance with two grandmas of your choice and you'll be the family darling forever.

GROOM'S PARENTS: Smile, grit your teeth, agree to everything, and remember this is absolutely the last time you have to be such nice people.

CLERGY: If you'll add a formal "in-law bonding ritual" along with the nuptials, at least the couple would find out what to call them. As one mother-in-law told us, "Ten thousand times I've asked my daughter-in-law to call me Sue, and ten thousand times she has answered, 'Yes ma'am, Mrs. Thomas.'"

At my wedding, my lovely but nervous bride motioned for her father to hurry up down the aisle. In a not so quiet voice Dad muttered, "At a hundred dollars a step, I'll take as long as I please."

CAL WARLICK

BRIDE'S FATHER: If you schedule the wedding during monsoon season, be sure the band can play "Dancing in the Dark."

BRIDE'S MOTHER: Beware: some out-of-town relatives will be offended if you send them an invitation, because they know you know they can't come, and they think you expect a gift. Others will be offended if you *don't* invite them, because they want to know the family news. And no one ever ends up on the right list.

UNSUSPECTING COUPLE: When a catered-dinner-orchestra-dancing family marries a punch-and-cookies family, somebody's going to be surprised.

At my niece's wedding, the groom forgot the ring, her mother-in-law dropped the cake, the pipes burst and thirty uninvited relatives showed up and devoured the food. The marriage lasted six months.

Aunt Clara came late to the wedding. Instead of an apology she remarked, "If I were a rich relative, you would have waited."

When Uncle Leon got married, his wife's parents sent a check, naively suggesting that the young couple put it aside for a rainy day. Leon was no fool. He sprinkled a few drops on the window and cashed it immediately.

JUST MARRIED
8
CAL WARBICK

As part of his pastoral duties, my father visited inmates at Indiana State Penitentiary, taking as many parishioners as he could persuade. Thus my fiancé, Warren, was cajoled into joining Dad on his monthly sojourn.

Always curious about visitors, a burly prisoner quizzed Warren relentlessly. "Do you know Fast Eddie?" he growled. "He was from your town." Who wouldn't remember the town's most infamous citizen? But not knowing how his answer would affect his health, Warren pleaded innocent on all counts.

When the inmates told Dad they would like to come to the wedding, Dad cheerfully replied, "If you can get out, you're welcome to come."

We don't think anyone escaped in time, but Warren never did figure out how our nuptials received such excellent coverage in the prison newspaper.

We probably all would have enjoyed having both families together if we hadn't had the wedding that went along with it.

My mother's been married four times and my father's been married five times, and everybody's still friendly. But all my uncle Arthur could say about the wedding was, "That was *some* receiving line."

The only safe seating arrangement for a wedding dinner is a hundred tables for two.

My sister-in-law sobbed throughout her entire wedding, up the aisle, during the ceremony and back down the aisle. As she passed my folks, Dad whispered none too quietly, "He's my son and he's not that bad."

When my son got married, I told my daughter-in-law, "I will only give advice when you ask, but please ask, because I sure do have a lot available."

RIGHT BEFORE THE WEDDING Ellen had her hair done at Mr. Kenneth's, one of New York's most famous and expensive salons. The look of the day was carefree, natural and windblown, and Ellen looked radiant.

Her mother-in-law also spent the day at the beauty salon. Not Mr. Kenneth's, but Thelma's in Queens. Her hair was dyed, beehived and lacquered. When the two women met, her mother-in-law shook her head and sighed, "Oh, honey, you decided not to get your hair done. Well, don't fret, it looks nice that way too."

At my wedding my father-in-law said, "I am so thrilled you're marrying my daughter. *That* should stop the flow of fiancés through our house."

If you don't hug your daughter-in-law on her wedding day, you'd better shake hands and go to your corner.

My stepdaughter should have known something was wrong on her wedding night when she appeared in her gorgeous negligee, and her husband called her into the bathroom to tell her she left the cap off the toothpaste.

My sister-in-law thinks my brother is handsome. Lucky for him!

When Bob and I got engaged, his aunt the professional artist invited us to her apartment. "I've finished your wedding present," she beamed, "and it's somewhere in this room. Pick it out."

I looked excitedly at the abstract watercolors on the walls and the graceful sculptures overflowing her shelves and tables. Afraid to venture a guess, I finally prevailed upon her to point out our gift: two lovingly sculptured, semi-formless, decidedly ugly ceramic horsehead bookends.

For twenty-three years I hid my disappointment, but in five moves, even when a trucker dropped the box from the van, the damn things still won't break.

After their wedding my daughter and son-in-law couldn't recall a word the minister said, they were too nervous to eat a bite and the reception was a blur. So I paid for a $12,000 case of amnesia.

The argument about renting a tent for our backyard wedding resumed when it started raining.

My brother-in-law couldn't be a better brother if he were homemade.

My mother-in-law wore the same dress at my wedding that she wore at my wife's first wedding. She said, "It was good enough for her first wedding, it's good enough for yours." If she keeps bugging me, she'll get to wear it again.

When my daughter announced her elopement, she said, "Dad, I know you'll love Tim. His hair is short, his record is clean, and he's got all his teeth."

My sister-in-law married the son of Mayor Richard J. Daley's dentist and invited the Daleys to the wedding. The Daley family arrived in three black stretch limousines. When a big, strapping young man came into the choir loft, the elderly organist asked, "Did you bring the music, and which love songs are you going to sing?" Patting his holster, the man boomed, "Lady, I'm the mayor's bodyguard, and I ain't gonna sing nothin'!"

My brother told his bride, "If we ever have an argument, I could never win. Your mother would take your side, and *my* mother would take your side."

My sister-in-law, the morning person, starts humming at 5 a.m. And my brother, the night person, wants to boogie at midnight. Their marriage is going to be one long day.

My society friend, Caroline, bragged about her daughter's fiancé: "We think it will make a nice little first marriage for her."

When Margaret's brother got married, everyone pitched in, bringing everything from the flowers to the food. The only bakery item was an expensive wedding cake that her sister-in-law couldn't afford but wouldn't do without.

After the church reception, the bride asked Margaret to freeze the top layer of the cake for their first anniversary. And there it sat, complete with bride and groom, for 357 days, until the week Margaret left town and the freezer broke.

Margaret's husband pronounced the freezer more disgusting than anything he had ever seen at medical school, and she was frantic. What should she do about the dead cake, reduced to bug-ridden rubble? With only two days left before the anniversary, Margaret dashed to the nearest bakery and begged them to "forge" the top layer of a wedding cake.

On the day of my wedding, my father-in-law shocked me by whispering, "Never be too tired." Thanks to him, after thirty years of marriage, I've worn out my husband.

CAL WARLICK

The next day, grabbing the sealed box, she arrived just in time for the party. Her sister-in-law and brother attributed the mutant hue of the roses to freezer burn, but they never could account for the toy groom's Jewish skull cap.

On penalty of having my fingernails pulled out, I will never let on to my son that I arranged for him to "accidentally" meet the girl he married.

With in-laws around, no wonder the guy who marries you is called a "justice of the peace." But where is he when you really need him?

When we announced our engagement, my mother-in-law greeted me with a hug and sighed with relief, "This is the day I've been praying for. At last I can get his stuff out of the house."

Right before his sister's wedding, Steve asked the groom, "Now that I'm almost your brother-in-law, how soon can I sleep on your couch and drink your good Scotch?"

As a wedding present, my in-laws commissioned the renowned photographer, Paul Gittings, to take our portrait. After posing us in the den and living room, he then suggested we adjourn to the porch.

When Mom protested that it was in no condition to be included in a portrait, he said, "Go get the broom," whereupon the famous artist started sweeping our front porch. "Oh," teased Mom, "I do hope the neighbors are impressed with the quality of our yard man." Grinning, he replied, "Wait till you tell them what you paid for it!"

You can't help but love someone who's crazy enough to marry your son the Tibetan history scholar.

My parents-in-law love their son. I benefit from the fallout.

When a family of huggers marries a family of crossed arms, the introductions take a while.

Just before Stan and Jenny left on their honeymoon, his father-in-law took him aside. "Stan, marriage is not easy. But if ever my daughter doesn't suit you, don't ever lay a hand on her. Just put her on a train for home. It doesn't have to be a compartment first class, just send her back to me." And Stan replied, "Yes, sir, I've got that."

As the wedding couple got into the car, Jenny's dad leaned into the window and whispered, "On second thought, you better make it Pullman."

CHAPTER 2

SOMETHING OLD, SOMETHING NEW, SOMETHING BORROWED, SOMETHING BLUE. . . AND THEY'RE ALL RELATIVES

(Getting to Know You)

ALPERN & BLUMENFELD'S FIRST THEORY OF RELATIVITY: On that enchanted evening when you see a stranger across a crowded room, you will never notice his family standing behind him.

Only after the honeymoon will you wonder, "Where did all these people come from?" And slowly you will begin to realize that marriage is like those Japanese Ginzu knife commercials. When you say yes to marrying your perfect mate, for no money extra you get a second pair of razor-sharp parents, ready-made siblings and a complete set of assorted cousins marked "irregular" with lifetime guarantees to wear out their welcome but never wear out.

To survive the first impression jitters, it's best to learn as much about in-law dynamics as possible ahead of time: Who is the real power in the family? Who's only a figurehead? Where do the unspoken alliances lurk? And whom should you not mention to whom?

But the biggest surprise of all, whether your in-laws are awe-inspiring or awful, is revealed in Alpern & Blumenfeld's Second Theory of Relativity: No matter how mature your marriage partner appears, a mere ten minutes with your in-laws will transform your spouse into an eight-year-old child (twelve if you're lucky). Gird your loins, it's inescapable. Even when Eleanor Roosevelt's husband, Franklin, had his hand on the front doorknob of the White House, her formidable mother-in-law never failed to nudge him day after day, "But, Franklin, don't you think you'll be cold going out without a coat?"

So on your first encounter with the other side, never forget Alpern & Blumenfeld's Third Theory of Relativity: Act normal in front of the in-laws. Your turn will come.

Meeting my in-laws for the first time is like a pony show. You go from house to house, tell them who you are, eat a little chicken, and tap out your age with your hoof.

If I had met my husband's brother before I met my husband, I would have married him instead. He's exactly like my husband, only nice.

When my in-laws try to hide their disapproval, I can always see through the tact to the fact.

My father-in-law was born assertive. What he needs now is a little submissiveness training, and the world would give thanks.

Your father-in-law's greatest joy is eating a good meal. My greatest joy is not having to cook it.

It was my first dinner with my wife's parents. While my mother-in-law went to check on the coffee, my father-in-law accidentally spilled a beet on their new white carpeting. As Mom entered the room, Dad patted me on the shoulder and said, "Don't worry, Matt, she won't mind a bit."

When Myrtle from Mobile was asked how her Yankee son-in-law adjusted to living in Alabama, she replied, "He was slow to begin with and he fits right in."

The day my sister got her own American Express card, my brother-in-law became a broke and disillusioned man.

My mother-in-law has eight children, and I am her third son's second wife. She hardly knows I'm there.

My brother-in-law has a great sense of humor if you love him and aren't easily offended.

How can I tell my dear mother-in-law to mind her own business when she's convinced I *am* her own business?

I will treat you as my own child. I will tell you what to do and how to do it. But if you're anything like my own children, you'll listen politely and then do whatever you bloody well please.

My in-laws' idea of a good time is taking a nap—preferably in separate rooms.

It's a family trait of my in-laws. All the women's hair turns blonde at forty.

How can my brother-in-law spend one hour at the Grand Canyon and come back with six hours worth of slides?

I knew I was accepted into the family the day my mother-in-law fed me leftovers.

UNCLE FRED, A SHOE SALESMAN, was a shy, well-mannered man but didn't have much business sense. He married a woman whose father later died and left them $40 million.

THE GRAND CANYON
CAL WARBICK

They began collecting art. One summer they went to Europe and, after much agonizing, purchased a painting for $250,000.

When they told Fred's sister-in-law what they had done, she gasped, "Fred, you two act just like nouveau riches." To which her soft-spoken brother-in-law replied, "Well, what in the hell do you think we are?"

My sister-in-law was worth $3 million *before* anyone died.

My mother-in-law will never say anything bad about someone unless she has proof. Then stand back and watch her burn up the telephone wires!

Why is it that my father-in-law remembers every bad joke he ever heard, but forgets he's already told it to me twice?

Whenever my mother-in-law wants to be assertive, she wears a power hat. The secret to winning an argument with her is to wear a bigger hat.

My sister-in-law can keep a secret better than anyone I know because she can't remember what she didn't listen to in the first place.

I sent my mother-in-law Fruit-of-the-Month. So now in addition to the fruit, she has a complaint every month.

SHORTLY AFTER WAYNE MARRIED into a prominent Texas family, his wheeler-dealer father-in-law moseyed into Wayne's tiny new law

CAL WARLICK

DON'T GET MAD
OUT LIVE THEM
AND EAT ALOT
AT THEIR WAKE
CAL WARLICK

office, puffing on a big cigar. "Well, Wayne, I just sold an apartment complex for $2 1/2 million."

"Wow," Wayne gasped, "congratulations on such a big sale."

"Yep," twanged his father-in-law, "every little 2 1/2 million sure helps!"

After ten years of marriage, my brother-in-law finally said, "Stan, I don't like people who pry, and you don't have to answer, but just exactly what do you do?"

I try to hug my mother-in-law at least once a year.

When my brother was an infant, only Mother knew what he was babbling about. Now that's my sister-in-law's job.

My father-in-law lived to be 102. His motto was, Don't get mad, outlive them . . . and eat a lot at their wake.

My brother-in-law is like postnasal drip. Not serious, but irritating.

Downwind from every Nobel Prize winner stands an amazed mother-in-law.

From the day karen graduated law school to the day she landed a job with a prestigious firm, her mother-in-law begged to see her in action. Finally Karen got up enough nerve to invite her to court. Every day her mother-in-law sat transfixed as Karen argued her case. On the final day, after a brilliant summation, the jury acquitted her client.

Triumphantly Karen escorted her mother-in-law out of the courtroom and asked, "Well, Ma, what did you think?" Looking at her adoringly, her mother-in-law replied, "Oh, honey, I loved the way the lights glinted off your hair."

CHAPTER 3

HAPPY DAYS—
YOU SHOULD LIVE SO LONG

(The Good Times)

FAMILY GATHERINGS ARE A TIME TO RENEW FRIENDSHIPS, rekindle a sense of history, and re-awaken dormant hostilities. All the ingredients are there: boisterous children, Cousin Ethel's lethal potato salad and the assemblage of random personalities bound only by a slender thread of DNA.

Holidays and reunions can be joyous occasions of genuine conviviality. But if you're just one of the in-laws surrounded by your spouse's rambunctious relatives, you have no "in" jokes, little shared history to "remember the time that," and way too much déjà vu. And you'd better not leave home without an up-to-date scorecard of who is talking to whom, so you won't blurt out Uncle Arthur's hilarious hunting story to his brother Bradley before Bradley's stitches have been removed.

Survival comes in many guises. You might curl up in a corner with the Sunday paper, or spend three glorious hours hiding in the kitchen making sure the chili doesn't stick. Still, family get-togethers ought to be recorded for posterity, so why not elect yourself family photographer? You'll be triply blessed with a mission, a wide-angle camera lens to hide behind, and an excuse not to linger over Cousin Nell's "So why aren't you pregnant yet?"

Since you're the "keeper of the memories," you'll have the fun of creating a scrapbook complete with captions—the ultimate revenge.

And if your father-in-law ever asks where you are in the album, just point to the last photo in the book: the classic picture of the whole kit and kaboodle lined up outdoors with 14 babies, 83 1/2 big smiles, and your giant thumb smack dab over Uncle Willie's face.

Whichever child has behaved the worst that year has to attend the family reunion with us.

When we were dating, my future husband's grandmother cornered me on New Year's Eve: "If you want a good man, marry my Patrick. You want good looks, buy goldfish."

Never seat your mother-in-law at the "B" table of the holiday dinner.

For twenty years, whenever we celebrate a happy family occasion, my parents-in-law are amazed they lived long enough to enjoy it.

After meeting my husband's long lost uncle, I can understand why they lost him.

I was twenty-four when I married a thirty-year-old man. My nephew-in-law was twenty-two and better looking than my husband. Imagine how I felt when we first met: he threw open his arms and crushed me to his manly chest yelling, "Auntie Marsha, Auntie Marsha, did you bring me a present?"

My in-laws always give surprise parties. The tradition is, you always know about it ahead of time, and you pretend to be surprised.

Aunt Lilly's memory fails until you don't show up at the family reunion.

Louise's future son-in-law gave her two Christmas presents. "When I opened the first, I said, 'Oh, Logan, homemade chunky peanut butter,' and popped a fingerful into my mouth. It tasted a bit odd, but then so was the look on Logan's face. Then I opened the other present: a nifty birdfeeder to hold the peanut butter/ birdseed glop."

After one glass of champagne, Ida's mother-in-law patted Ida's hand and said, "It's so lovely to get together for Christmas dinner, even though we can't stand each other the rest of the year."

Uncle Charlie fancies himself the family historian. The year he researched that we were related to Richard Nixon, the Democratic branch of the family almost split for good.

Surrounded by in-laws at Thanksgiving, I know why Dorothy clicked her heels and said, "There's no place like home. There's no place like home."

My mother-in-law is an is-it-too-hot-is-it-too-cold-is-it-really-OK-do-you-really-like-it cook.

When my folks first met Dawn's folks on Valentine's Day, they all went to a restaurant. My father said, "Now that we're here, let's get acquainted." Her father said, "Now that we're here, let's eat."

Passover dinner at my in-laws means kids, laughter, a long religious service, and a case of indigestion you can only get from 3,000-year-old recipes.

If you have to insult your in-laws, do it with a laugh. Chances are, they'll laugh right along with you and won't recognize the insult until you're long gone.

It was Cheryl's turn for Thanksgiving dinner, and she didn't look forward to hosting her unsociable brother-in-law. Sure enough, after Bill ate his meal in silence, he retired to the den to read a book for two hours, leaving the other guests to sit and gab. As everyone packed up their casseroles to leave, Bill murmured appreciatively, "Thanks for the dinner, Cheryl, it's been a pleasure not talking to you."

After meeting Charlotte's three brothers-in-law at the family reunion, I realized she got the pick of the litter.

Give me a superficially polite son-in-law any day. Who cares what they really think?

Family reunions are fun if you have a large family and don't have to talk to any one person for more than three minutes.

My father-in-law has only one talent. At birthday parties he can balance a full martini glass on his head and dance the tango.

When I told my friend Tony everyone in the family wants my mother-in-law at holiday time, he offered me his mother-in-law, his Porsche, and his forty year collection of baseball cards in trade.

REUNION

After his parents-in-law returned from their first family reunion in over fifty years, Bob said to his mother-in-law, "I didn't think you had enough cousins who speak to each other to hold a family reunion." "Well," she sighed, "it turns out Arthur invited only the relatives he wanted to see . . . all five of us."

When I die it had better be on Christmas, because my mother-in-law would never take off work just to come to my funeral.

I have had four heart attacks and two surgeries, but I was never lucky enough for them to happen in time to miss the family reunion.

When my wife's six aunts gather in the kitchen to cook Thanksgiving dinner, it's bumper-to-bumper bosoms.

When our family goes out for an Easter all-you-can-eat buffet, my brother-in-law surveys the feast and then announces, "Everyone go home. I can handle this myself."

At holiday reunions the men go into one room to brag about their accomplishments and the women go into another room to tell the truth.

Susan put her son, Eric, in the playpen and spent six hours cleaning the house for her in-laws' visit. Later, surveying her gleaming home, she cooed, "I'm sorry it's not perfect." To which her Boston-bred mother-in-law replied, "That's all right, we turn our heads."

How come, when they drive you nuts, it's still sad to say goodbye?

When we all get together, my mother-in-law and my wife both love to talk. In thirty-seven years, I haven't gotten in more than a thousand words, and believe me I was lucky at that!

My brother-in-law found a vacation spot halfway between our homes. He drives five hours to get there and we drive ten. That's what poor math, a good tailwind and a soft touch can get you.

This year I'm declaring In-law Amnesty Day. All past transgressions and overdue apologies will be forgiven, and we can all start over with a clean slate.

One Christmas morning, with her mother-in-law in attendance, Frances unwrapped her husband's gift—a camera. Seeing it, her mother-in-law beamed, "Oh, Frances, I'm so glad he gave you a Polaroid. I understand any idiot can learn to use it!"

CHAPTER 4

THINGS WE WOULD NEVER PUT IN THIS BOOK

(The Not-So-Good Times)

IF YOU HAVE A RELATIVE with the disposition of a rattlesnake, who's so cantankerous that a sheepdog won't go near him, then you are the sorry kinsman of a family "outlaw."

Bilious of eye and caustic of tongue, the in-law desperado is always out there looking for a gum fight. And being the cowardly bushwhacker that he is, he usually fires from the lip at you and your amiable sidekick, when you least expect it.

So what's the best way to deal with the nastiest inherited relative west of the Pecos? Sheriff John Slaughter, a man of few words, cleaned up Tombstone, Arizona, in the 1800s by recommending, "Shoot first and yell 'Throw up your hands' afterwards." But since most of us don't enjoy stirring our soup with the barrel of a six shooter, and we may have to account for our own actions on Judgment Day, perhaps there are some better signposts to follow while you mosey down the in-law/outlaw trail.

Thunder and lightning are the biggest cause of a stampede. So when that in-law/outlaw shoots off some verbal fireballs of wrath, don't get spooked. Keep your mouth shut and hang close to the herd. And when you ride into camp, stay downwind so you won't kick up a lot of dust.

Do not strew your bedroll near the family outlaw's personal domain, where it can be stumbled over. And most importantly, if you want warmth, don't whittle away your time poking at the outlaw's cold embers. Collect your own wood, build your own warming fire and, whatever you do, never shout, "Hombre, you've been alookin' fer a fight? Now you kin have it."

My mother-in-law has the motive and the weapon, but fortunately since she lives in Australia she's never had the opportunity.

Logic gets on my sister-in-law's nerves.

In a world of tropical flowers, my father-in-law is an iguana.

Whenever I get mad at my husband, I yell, "How could such nice people have a son like you?"

When your son-in-law spoils your daughter you say, "Isn't he a gem." When your son spoils your daughter-in-law, you say, "Isn't she a brat!"

CAL WARLICK

The secret to being a good in-law is, never ask them to lift a finger. As if they would.

My sister-in-law's tongue is so sharp she could lick the icing off the cake and leave the candles burning.

Whenever my husband's grandfather became ill, he was sure he would die. He would call the children into the bedroom and tearfully divide his few belongings among them. And each time he recovered, he would quickly call another gathering to recoup their temporary windfall.

When I first met my in-laws I was dully impressed.

Helene sent out a notice of her divorce: "Helene G___ wishes to announce her recent divorce and thanks her many in-laws who helped make this glorious event possible."

My sister-in-law the kindergarten teacher is like a peanut butter and jelly sandwich with too much jelly.

The first time my mother-in-law came to visit she told me, "You're doing pretty well, considering your background."

In a family that sews, quilts, bakes, builds and tinkers, my son-in-law can't stir soup.

SMACK
SMACK
SMACK
SMACK
SMACK
CAL WARLICK

My brother-in-law wasn't on speaking terms with anyone in the family, so no one knew he was alive until he died.

Having in-laws means learning more than you ever wanted to know.

When Hurricane Gilbert forced everyone in Galveston to evacuate, Buck drove his very pregnant wife to his mother-in-law's house in Dallas. When his wife inquired, "Are you staying?" Buck considered it a moment. "No," he concluded, "I'd rather go back and take my chances with Gilbert."

Nice people die and fade away. Mick's father-in-law was so mean, they are still talking about him.

As my sister-in-law Grace left a fancy party, the guest of honor thanked her for coming. Grace replied, "Oh, I'd go anywhere to see anybody if the food was good enough."

Here's the in-law final exam: When your kids are little, take a joint vacation with your in-laws to Mobile, Alabama, in July, rent a two-bedroom condo, and watch thirteen inches of rain fall in five days.

With all the warring factions in my wife's family, my father-in-law always manages to be Switzerland.

If you know the expression, "Have a nice day," you never met my brother-in-law.

My brother-in-law married a girl who was so universally disliked, the groomsmen even tried to talk him out of marrying her at their wedding.

When my Boston-bred husband brought me to meet my in-laws for the first time, he introduced me as a Protestant, vegetarian, divorcée potter from the South. My in-laws had a look on their faces that said, "Why don't you just kill us in our beds?"

My brother-in-law is a deep thinker. I assume that's what he's doing.

Have you ever walked your dog and had it stop in the middle of the street and refuse to budge? That's my mother-in-law.

Our first baby boy was born with brown hair and brown eyes. My mother-in-law's first reaction was, "The only one in our family with brown eyes is Ratzo the dog."

My daughter has a built-in jerk detector, which has led her unerringly to both of her ex-husbands.

TSK
TSK
MUMBLE
WELL, I THINK
THE
CAL WARLICK

Even after we've been married twenty years, my mother-in-law is still taking bets with the neighbors that it won't last.

DAVID, A MARRIAGE COUNSELOR, was weary of hearing his clients always blame each other for their problems. So he was surprised the day a client said that his spouse was only fifty percent to blame.

"At last," David thought, "here's someone who takes responsibility." Just then the client added, "The other half of the blame goes to my mother-in-law."

My relationship with my mother-in-law improves greatly when I turn down my hearing aid and nod in agreement.

Most people can make a good first impression if they really try hard, but don't expect them to keep it up for the next thirty years.

Every family has a member they don't like to talk about. Thank God, I'm it.

My father-in-law is a bother-in-law.

People aren't mean in-laws. They were rotten to begin with, and they're just being consistent.

I should have known something was wrong when my fiancé introduced me to his mother as she was peeling potatoes and she didn't look up.

I was dubious about meeting my wife's folks. The last thing I needed was another set of adults who didn't think I was ambitious enough.

My mother-in-law is the Jeanne Dixon of negative predictions.

KAREN'S IN-LAWS WENT TO THEIR LAWYER to make out their wills. Every time the lawyer said, "If one of you dies. . ." her mother-in-law would blurt out, "God forbid!" This went on for over an hour, and the interruptions were making the lawyer lose both his place and his composure.

Finally, he sighed, "I'll tell you what. If I get my secretary to type up one big 'God forbid!' and I notarize it, will that last the rest of the afternoon?" To which she replied, "God willing."

CHAPTER 5

A ROSE IS A ROSE IS A ROSE, UNLESS YOU CALL IT A PETUNIA

(Kids)

IN THE DAYS OF LARGE FAMILIES, there were always enough wee ones to sprinkle on the family tree, naming babies after both sets of grandparents, a famous cousin, plus the odd aunt or two. But in today's family constellation of 2.1 children, the vise of familial pressure provokes many a "name-game" headache.

Will your in-laws be appeased if you promise the next baby to their branch of the family? Are there any laws against saddling an only child with "Mary Margaret Rankin Frances" to cover all your bases? So what if your last name is Stewart and naming him after Uncle Armand Stern the millionaire will give your bundle of joy a censorable monogram?

But concocting your sweet baby's name "Aida" from the grandparents' four initials only gets you over the first hurdle.

With a freshly-named baby in tow, dealing with both sides of the family will require the equipment handling of Mayflower, the juggling skill of Doug Henning, and the diplomacy of Henry Kissinger.

If you let the baby spend five hours with one set of grandparents, you'd better not let her spend five hours and ten minutes with the other set. Even if you divide your time down to the last nanosecond, it isn't equal. Your mom got custody of a dozing baby, while your mother-in-law got custody right after breakfast. Your dad greeted your arrival at 2 a.m. with a loaded video recorder and a yell to "Smile for Grandpa!" Your father-in-law greeted you with a completed college application to his alma mater. Aunts and uncles arrived two hours late and missed Saturday's baby allotment altogether. The only sane solution . . . there is no sane solution. But eventually they grow up.

And so do the children.

My mother-in-law can sniff out a family pregnancy faster than a bird dog can flush a quail.

Nine months and one day after I married Louise, my father-in-law came over and congratulated us because my pregnant wife hadn't given birth yet.

PENNY WAS IN LABOR WITH HER FIRST CHILD, and the expectant father was looking forward to being in the delivery room. His parents rushed to the hospital to share the momentous occasion.

After many hours of difficult labor, the doctor decided to do

CAL WARLICK

a Caesarian section. As the nurses wheeled Penny into the operating room with her husband at her side, his parents waylaid the obstetrician and pleaded, "Doctor, take care of our son in there!"

The only thing my ex-father-in-law doesn't like about his granddaughter is that she looks like me. So he's stuck with my face, and that gives me a lot of pleasure.

When my children ask Grandpa to play catch, he replies, "I don't bend in as many places as I used to."

My mother-in-law couldn't think of one single soul in her family she'd want us to name our child after.

ON MY SON'S FIRST BIRTHDAY my father-in-law said, "Nancy, I want to thank you for naming him after Uncle Sam." Uncle Sam? I thought. Who in God's name was Uncle Sam?

I later asked my husband; he didn't know. To this day, we have no idea who Uncle Sam was. But it didn't matter then, and it doesn't matter now. There was peace in the family.

If it's the family's first grandchild, you have to realize that you've been chosen to train the grandparents for the rest of the children to come.

My in-laws take our five kids to their apartment pool and leave them until they shrivel up.

A daughter-in-law is someone who wasn't good enough to marry your son, but whose children are the most wonderful people in the world.

Virginia remembers her baby's birth as if it were yesterday. "In the hospital, when I learned I just had a boy, I said, 'When he grows up, I hope he finds a nice girl and settles down.' My mother-in-law replied, 'When he grows up, he'll take up with any old thing he wants to and you'll have nothing to say about it. Believe me, I know.'"

My sister-in-law announced that the day her obstetrician retired, so did she.

My son loves my mother-in-law. She bakes cookies, knits sweaters, and always returns his motorcycle in good condition.

Every April 15th, my twelve-year-old son wants to visit my father-in-law so he can impress his friends with the new cuss words he's learned.

Chips
CARL WARLICK©

My brother-in-law, Harold, a doctor at the Centers for Disease Control, was helping at his son's nursery school on Parents' Day. When a child smacked his head on the swing and produced a huge bump, the teachers frantically shouted for my brother-in-law.

Harold gave the boy a big kiss on his forehead, said, "All better," then whispered to the teacher, "What do I know? I'm in V.D."

Smile when your father-in-law says, "Michael Jr. will love becoming a Clemson Tiger like me."

A picnic with your grandchildren is no picnic.

If you don't know what to call your mother-in-law, have a baby. Then you can call her Grandma.

I can keep quiet when my daughter and son-in-law argue. And when they spend money they don't have. But when my grandchildren throw tantrums in a restaurant and neither parent says a word, my mother-in-law volcano erupts.

When you name your baby after someone in the family, the peace is short-lived and only lasts until the next child is born.

One grandpa takes our son fishing and the other grandpa takes him to watch the stockbroker's board. With those genes, he'll end up being an angler who knows all the angles.

With Aunt Mildred's gifts it's always a challenge to be grateful. Once, when she came to visit, she brought my children a game of jacks. John got the ball, Mitch got the jacks and Henry got the pencil to keep score.

When my brother, my sister-in-law and their children come for dinner, group rigor mortis sets in immediately after dessert and doesn't go away until they hear the dishwasher click on.

My mother-in-law was born with a manicure and a butler. So it comes naturally to her, when she sees me with three babies hanging off me while I'm stirring the soup, to take one look and say, "Well, if there's nothing else I can do, I'll go read a book."

My fifteen-year-old granddaughter has so much energy and talks so fast that we have to nap after her visits until the words stop bouncing off the walls.

My in-laws have five children and eight grandchildren, so Pop's idea of heaven is an empty house, Mozart and a pizza to call his own.

When Helen's daughter-in-law told Helen and John of the birth of their granddaughter, John sighed, "Last night I went to bed with my sweetheart, and this morning I'm in the sack with Grandma."

CAL WARLICK

Jenny and Stan named their daughter after her mother, so after that of course the child could do no wrong. No matter what she did, Grandma would say, "That is perfectly all right."

Once, two-year-old Sally was trying to pick up a cup from the table. Grandma kept saying, "Pick it up, darlin', pick it up." Sally finally dropped it, and it broke. "That's OK," Grandma reassured her daughter and son-in-law, "I read somewhere that it takes more control to let it go than it does to pick it up. So you see, she is even smarter than we thought."

Chapter 6

MY BROTHER-IN-LAW THE ELEPHANT WASHER & OTHER RARE BIRDS

(Resigned to the Bizarre)

Every family has at least one member who's a strange duck, and chances are this nonconformist is the relative they don't tell you about until after the wedding.

Perhaps someone did mention that your wife's uncle Hubert dabbles in oils, but most likely you will have to discover for yourself that he does it in the nude. And yes, it is true that your husband's cousin, Illona, has a pet. But why didn't anyone tell you it's a seven-foot boa constrictor with a fondness for redheads?

Whether misfits bewitch or bother, those unconventional relatives are bound to bewilder. How do you respond when your mother-in-law brings you a garland of garlic as a housewarming gift? When your wife announces that her anniversary present is a trip to the Himalayas to meet her long lost brother, Bubba? And your scientist father-in-law, Victor, declares over the vichyssoise, "Think of it! The brain of a dead man waiting to live again in a body I made with my own two hands!"

Admit it! These folks just don't fit. But take heart. With the bizarre, what's a misfit in one family is a fit in another. Sure enough, what you find a bit unusual will probably be considered perfectly normal behavior by that weird family down the block.

And whether you like it or not, your unconventional relatives will never fail to perform the unexpected when you have company, are virtually indestructable, and will always provide an inexhaustable source of gossip to liven up the rest of the family.

Leara's first mother-in-law loved to picnic at the cemetery. She said it was quiet, no Frisbees, and there was always a flat surface to put the potato salad.

My father-in-law has to run through the names of his two ex-wives and his three pit bulls before he can get my name right.

My teenaged brother-in-law loves monster movies. He likes to be with his own kind.

I love my sister-in-law. It's my brother I can't stand.

Marilyn was introduced to my brother, Neal, in London and then left for Copenhagen the next day. After corresponding for one year, Neal proposed. Marilyn flew back, and two weeks later they were married. After their honeymoon, Marilyn confided to me that she still hated her wedding band. "Why don't you just tell him?" I suggested. "Oh, my goodness," Marilyn said, "I don't know him well enough!"

At the open-casket funeral of my friend, her sister-in-law said to the family: "Oh, I love the way Jean's hair looks. Where did she get it done?"

Why is it that my mother-in-law is never on speaking terms with any of her relatives, but she always has a cousin for us to call when we go on vacation?

Every time I fix my bullheaded brother-in-law up with one of my girlfriends, he borrows his Dad's pickup and leaves his Porsche at home.

My sister-in-law and I have the same name, but she has a wild reputation. So I get all the blame and she has all the fun.

My dad's sister, Aunt Ruth, who was as flat as an ironing board, wanted to look more voluptuous but was embarrassed to buy falsies. So my generously endowed mother volunteered to get them for her. When she got to Woolworth's and asked for falsies, the saleslady blurted out, "You don't need any." Whereupon Mother replied, "I know. They're for my sister-in-law." "OK, what size do you want?" the saleslady asked. Having no experience in this area, Mom looked around and finally decided. "I think I'll take the size of the cashier. Thank you very much."

My husband admits that his relatives are crazy. Fortunately, they also have difficulty finding people willing to marry them, so in another generation the family might be normal.

Matilda thinks her in-laws don't like her, just because they replaced all the pictures in the wedding album with those of her husband and his former fiancée.

Every spring in Amherst, Massachusetts, my mother-in-law halts traffic to help salamanders cross the road.

How do you tell people your brother-in-law is a professional elephant washer?

Everyone calls my brother-in-law Grumplestiltskin.

Some people collect stamps and others collect coins, but my husband's Uncle Bill, the oral surgeon, built a whole room around his collection of mounted teeth.

CAL WARLICK

My husband has a first cousin twice removed, but he keeps coming back.

Really nervous about meeting my fiancée's family, I was totally unprepared for Joy's uncle Howard, who boasted that I was marrying into a family of historic lineage: "Why there's even a town in Massachusetts named after your fiancée's great grandfather." I marveled, "Really? Which one?" "Marblehead," he replied.

My older daughter's hubby is a terrific fellow but has little ambition, while my younger daughter's husband is intelligent and high-powered, but self-centered. Combined they'd make one sensational son-in-law. If only I could send the leftovers home.

Where can I trade in my shortsighted son for the wonderful woman he divorced?

When my sister-in-law returned to work, my brother claimed she made the kitchen smaller and put in vending machines.

My wife's uncle the artist gets $2,000 for a painting. When he showed us his latest abstract in shades of brown, titled "The Farm," all I saw was the manure.

My mother's friend Louise phoned excitedly: "Ruth, come see the latest slasher movie with me. My new daughter-in-law 's the third body from the right."

VEND
FOR
YOURSELF
ICE
TEA
COFFEE
SOFT
DRINK
CAL WARLICK

My sister-in-law is an actress. But when she won a part in the play, *Cabaret*, I had trouble picturing my shy relative in the role of a prostitute. After watching her opening night performance, I asked, "How can you play the romantic scene with the sailor so convincingly?" "Oh," she confided, "when I look at him, instead of seeing a man, I conjure up a picture of Beef Wellington, and I immediately start drooling. Works every time!"

When Sally B's sister-in-law broke her leg, before she would go to the hospital, she dragged herself into the bathroom to shave her legs and paint her toenails.

My father-in-law keeps a file called, "Things to Do." That's where he files everything he never does.

My friends are totally unsympathetic when I tell them that my mother-in-law drives me crazy showering me with compliments.

Every time my sister-in-law gives us a gaudy gift, we put it in our motor home and lose it across America.

My mother is a hypochondriac and my mother-in-law is a Christian Scientist. So when I have a headache, one will tell me to will it away and the other will tell me I've got a brain tumor.

My mother-in-law told me, "I'm not a babysitter, so don't ask me." I didn't. Now she calls my girlfriend in Texas and begs, "Can I stay with your kids?"

My in-laws are so dense I could write a book about them and not use pseudonyms.

During a bus strike in Minneapolis, Albert's elderly grandmother-in-law needed to get a prescription from the drugstore. She thought about her predicament and then called the only undertaker she knew. "Please send one of your cars for me." When he replied that it couldn't be done, she asked, "Would you pick me up if I were dead?" He said, "Of, course." "Well, I am still alive," she snapped, "and I'd appreciate your help more now than later." Everyone at the drugstore stared as Granny jumped out of the hearse. And the prescription was filled much faster than usual.

The first time I met my three-year-old brother-in-law, Wilson, he picked me a bunch of daffodils and then ran into the woods and threw rocks at me.

When my mother-in-law showed me her latest purchase—two silver candlesticks attached to china cherubs with crystal belly-buttons—my reaction came from a young bride's need to please: "Oh, Mother Madison, that just fits in here perfectly!"

My brother-in-law is a diamond in the rough—a lot of rough.

One evening my new daughter-in-law made beef stew for several friends. When my son walked in the door late and asked, "Is there any food left for me?" she gasped, "Oh, it's you . . . I forgot I was married."

When my sister-in-law Sally got engaged, she eagerly described her future father-in-law, a noted historian, to her family. "Bert's dad is eighty-nine years old, and he still delivers papers all over the country." "Oh, the poor man," sighed her grandmother, "I hope at least it's **The Wall Street Journal*!"***

CHAPTER 7

OH, LORD, I THINK I LIKE MY IN-LAWS

THERE IT WAS AT THE GROCERY STORE checkout counter, one of those newspapers. You know, the kind that screams, "I'm a disreputable sleaze. Buy me!" This one had three headlines: "Possum cheats death inches from expressway ramp," "Elvis sighted gyrating in pink UFO," and "Woman discovered who likes her in-laws."

In the photos, the possum looked more shaken than Elvis. And the in-law-liking woman from Butte, Montana? Well, she didn't look much different from the rest of us. Her name was Harriett, and hers was a simple but telling tale.

"The first time I was invited to my future mother-in-law's house for dinner, I had to get dressed up. I wore a fancy black dress with a rhinestone buckle in the back. Mom had antique mahogany chairs. When I stood up, the buckle scratched the back of my chair. My mother-in-law never said, Boo! Now, forty years later, whenever my mother-in-law leaves her teeth on the counter, I say to myself, 'Remember the buckle. Remember the buckle.'"

Harriett has now formed "In-law Lovers Anonymous," whose burgeoning membership audaciously tackles one of the last remaining taboos in civilized Western society: in-law liking.

"'Remember the buckle' has become our rallying cry," she says, "and we work passionately toward the day when it will finally be socially acceptable to hang a crewel sampler in every American living room with the words, 'Love Thy In-laws as Thyself.'"

While interviewing people for this book, we didn't run across any possum or spy Elvis in his chauffered UFO, but we did meet several members of In-Law Lovers Anonymous. A tenacious bunch, they were hard to shake as they insisted on sharing their stories. Believe it, plenty of people out there like their in-laws. But none so fervently as the woman who told us, "I was married three times and loved all my in-laws . . . it was their sons I couldn't stand."

I like having a son-in-law. When my wife complains that I watch too much football, I claim it's a male bonding thing, and make him sit there until she goes away.

On our fifth anniversary, my mother-in-law finally gave me her secret recipe for chocolate soufflé. With a hug, she whispered, "After putting up with my son for five years, now I know you have the patience to wait for the soufflé to rise."

CAL WARLICK

CAL WARLICK

My father-in-law has proof that Coca-Cola Classic is not the original formula. "For twenty years I'd clean my windshield with a bottle of Coke and it would stay clean. With Coke Classic the film comes back in a couple of days."

I love my mother-in-law because she believes I can do anything.

When she becomes famous, the fourth cousin once removed of your sister-in-law's aunt, who years ago divorced the uncle—is all of a sudden a very close relative.

My brother-in-law has nothing to say, but he does it so well.

My daughter-in-law and I have so much in common. We get mad at my son for the same reasons.

When I first met my mother-in-law, I thought, "No one can be that nice all the time," and for twenty-five years now she's proven me wrong.

My dear mother-in-law never blames me for cooking a rotten meal, but you should hear what she says about the butcher.

My father-in-law tells the same family stories over and over. When the kids say, "Grandpa, you've told us that story before, " he'll smile sweetly and say, "It bears repeating."

I knew I loved my sister-in-law when she squashed a roach in my kitchen and didn't tell a soul.

My mother-in-law always says, "It's better to tell the truth and have people say, 'I didn't realize you were that old,' than to lie, and have them say, 'My, doesn't she look old for her age.'"

I melt every time my son-in-law says he hopes his wife will turn out exactly like me.

Where I come from, you're trained from birth to love your in-laws even if you hate them.

My father-in-law is hard of hearing. When he asked, "What did you say?" people replied, "Never mind, it doesn't matter, it's not important." When Dad got his hearing aid, he said, "You know, they were right."

I knew my in-laws were my best friends when my wife and I didn't hear about the kids' chicken pox or the gerbil's funeral until after we returned home from our romantic vacation for two.

My daughter-in-law tells me to spend their inheritance on a trip around the world, and she means it.

Sometimes the only redeeming quality my husband has are his parents.

My daughter-in-law asked her internist if he could recommend a good orthopedic specialist. He said, "Yes, I recommend the doctor who operated on my mother-in-law's hip." She paused and then asked, "Doctor, I have another question. Do you like your mother-in-law?"

Sometimes I forget and think that *he's* my son, and *you're* my daughter-in-law.

My mother-in-law and I don't like the wind in our hair or the sand in our shoes. Just let us shop anywhere in the world and we're happy.

Whenever I call, my mother-in-law asks me if I'm calling from my car phone. If I say yes, Mom slams down the phone so her favorite daughter-in-law will keep both hands on the wheel.

My father-in-law has a selective memory. That's why leftovers are always a pleasant surprise.

I knew I loved my mother-in-law the moment she threw up her hands and said, "If I don't make my grandchildren behave, they wreck my house. If I do make them behave, the other grandmother is the good grandmother."

The secret to staying married for twenty-five years is that I like my in-laws. I don't have the heart to stick them with their son again.

When Dr. Ruth asked my seventy-eight-year-old father-in-law, "Do you watch my program?" he replied, "Yes, my wife and I lie in bed, watch your program, and reminisce."

According to my mother-in-law, my husband never did anything wrong, so therefore I must be OK.

I knew I loved my mother-in-law the day she introduced me to her friends as her "daughter-in-love."

My son-in-law is a grateful eater.

When Dian first married, she invited her in-laws over for dinner. Making her first pot of coffee, she carefully measured out two heaping tablespoons of coffee per cup. She confided, "After trying to stir their cups of sludge, no one brought it to their lips

Jenna and Martin, who run a business together, are typical parents of the '90s. Non-sexist in their lifestyle, they take turns cooking dinner for their family. But Jenna's mom feels sorry that her son-in law has to cook. "So when it's my turn," says Martin,"she often arrives with a meal on wheels. I always tell Jenna, if we ever get a divorce, the children won't be a problem. But I'll fight like hell for custody of your mother!"

CAL WARLICK

except my dear father-in-law, who drank it all up without saying a word. That's when I knew he was my friend."

My daughter-in-law is my best friend because, when we go shopping, she's the only one who will admit, "That dress makes you look like a freight train."

I knew I loved my father-in-law the day the two of us went to a movie together, and he blushed when a client spotted us and gave him the fish-eye for cavorting with a younger woman.

After being widowed for ten years, Min's fifty-year-old daughter-in-law finally started dating a very nice man. Gingerly she asked seventy-eight-year-old Min, "Mom, do you object?" Min replied, "Are you kidding? While you're at it, ask him if he knows someone for me."

If you ask my son-in-law, he'll tell you I'm wonderful, if he knows what's good for him.

I get along famously with my mother-in-law. I only speak English and Mama only speaks French, so when she phones, I say her granddaughter's name, shout "Bon!" and call my husband to the phone.

My father-in-law tells seventy years worth of jokes and my mother-in-law can't remember them for ten minutes. That adds up to fifty years of wedded bliss.

I knew I loved my in-laws when they told me they would protect me from my mother.

My mother-in-law was always there for me. She was right by my side when I learned to cook. She was right by my side when I needed a babysitter. And she was right by my side when I divorced the bum.

How can you not love a daughter-in-law when she thanks you for your son every year on his birthday?

THOUGH MY MOTHER-IN-LAW KEPT KOSHER, at lunchtime she didn't object to having meat and milk dishes on the table simultaneously to satisfy everyone's preferences, as long as no one put them on the same plate.

At the end of lunch there was one meatball sitting in a bowl. "Bobby," encouraged Mom, who never wasted anything, "Have the last meatball."

One by by this sweet lady tried to foist that meatball off on each of us. No takers. Unable to stand the thought of throwing it away, Mom finally reached over with her fork and impaled the meatball.

As we watched her eat it, Bob said in mock horror, "But, Mom, you're eating the meatball with your dairy lunch." His grey-haired mother smiled gently and replied, "That's OK, Bobby dear, these aren't my real teeth."

CHAPTER 8

ALL GOOD THINGS MUST END, AND NONE TOO SOON

(Visits)

IT MIGHT LEAVE A BAD IMPRESSION if you strip search your father-in-law to prevent him from smuggling cigars into your living room. Or if you refuse to discuss the meaning of life with your mother-in-law through the bathroom door. You have your own way of doing things. The problem is, so do your in-laws. When your in-laws do things their way on your turf, that can lead to a lot of sticky wickets.

Only one house in the United States has the proper guidelines for visitors—the White House in Washington, D.C. If only we could apply the First Family's rules to our own relatives, how simple in-law visits would become.

First of all, the time your in-laws spend inside your house would seem short compared with the time they spend lined up outside waiting to get in. Your wife's teenaged nieces and nephews would be required to check their decibel-blasting radios at the door. And you could, with a straight face, restrict visiting hours from 10 a.m. to 12 noon, Tuesday through Saturday. The family would only be allowed in five designated rooms, and would be required to stay on the plastic runner and out of the roped off areas.

Secondly, you could tell your brother-in-law, "No photos allowed. So leave your equipment at home." And best of all, your sister-in-law would have to accept the bipartisan edict to "glance at the knicknacks, but do not rearrange, dust, or touch."

As your in-laws enter, you could hand them a touching note modeled after one written by Patricia Nixon saying, "I wish you much pleasure in your visit and a quiet joy as you relive your moments with us. And please take home with you a memento of your stay, a souvenir booklet of warm family sentiments for only $3.95."

One thing for sure: If White House rules were imposed on your in-laws, there would be less talking, more listening, a lot of oohing and ahhing, and a fast, clean exit.

My husband and I both have jobs, five kids, three dogs, a cat and six rabbits, and my retired in-laws still insist it's easier when we come to visit them.

I love when my in-laws visit. My wife and I get along famously because she won't give her folks the satisfaction of seeing us argue.

CAL WARBICK

CAL WARLICK

My wife's ex-husband spends so much time over here with the kids that I call him my husband-in-law.

My daughter-in-law knew she was one of us when she arrived and the faded sheets were on the bed.

No matter how long we scrub, my father-in-law always says, "Nice place you have here. Could use a good cleaning."

When my mother-in-law says, "We are going to do yard work today," her heels, stockings and gloves are a tipoff that *we* aren't going to do anything. It means *I* am going to do yard work and *she* is going to say, "that goes here and this goes there."

When your mother-in-law comes to visit, put a welcome basket in the guest room with fresh flowers, fruit and a really good racy book.

Such a coincidence, my sister-in-law is always out when I come for a visit.

If your in-laws wanted you to know what they were saying, they would be speaking English.

My mother-in-law gave me a wonderful husband, and she never lets me forget it.

My father-in-law has a big heart, a sweet disposition and a ready laugh. My mother-in-law says it's hell to get mad at a man who has the whole family on his side.

My son-in-law wants me to leave him alone, but he wishes me excellent health while I'm doing it.

SHARA'S BEST FRIEND DOESN'T GET ALONG with her mother-in-law who was coming to visit. She grumbled, "My mother-in-law doesn't get along with anyone." Being in a positive action mode, Shara said, "Just a minute, I'll take care of this. Surely you can find one positive thing about her visit." Silence.

"How long is she staying?" Shara asked. "Well," her friend allowed, "she's leaving in three days." "See?" Shara roared triumphantly, "right away something good!"

It's a lot easier to laugh off your in-laws' quirks when you didn't have to spend your childhood under their spell.

Forgive and forget at least half of what your in-laws say, and save the rest for a rainy day.

If food were a religion, my brother-in-law would be president of the congregation.

If you want to see a smile on your father-in-law's face, always keep a joke book in the bathroom.

My husband and his folks bicker over everything. My in-laws always drop in when they know he won't be home, so they don't see him for months at a time. They'll say, "Oh, Greg will be home soon, we'd better leave."

Whenever I visit my mother-in-law, I have to peel myself off her plastic chair covers.

It's exhausting to out-bubble my mother-in-law.

MOTHER, WHOSE MEDICAL KNOWLEDGE IS SLIM, visited her friend, Pauline, recuperating from a hysterectomy. As she set a bouquet of flowers on the hospital dresser, Mom couldn't help noticing a large Mason jar with white tubular things floating in yellow fluid, with a bone sticking up. "Sakes alive, Pauline, is that your operation?"

"Oh, Ruth," Pauline roared. "That's chicken soup my mother-in-law made me, but there's no way I could ever eat it now!"

Power on power off, my father-in-law's favorite activity is sitting in front of the TV.

If I let my husband's Aunt Vivian come live with us like she wants to, there'll be plenty of room, because I'd kill myself and my husband would divorce me.

The only way to clean up my sister-in-law's office is toss in a grenade and slam the door quick.

You know your father-in-law has stayed too long when he starts reading the telephone book.

When small talk escalates, it's time to go home.

MY MOTHER-IN-LAW WAS A MODEST LADY and never acknowledged that, though we were married, her son and I shared the same bed. When we visited, she'd put each of us in a single bed—me on the third floor and her son on the second.

One night we drove to Lovers' Point. After a while a policeman drove up, shined his light into the window and asked why we were there. My husband said, "Officer, this lady is my wife and we are staying with my parents." The policeman said, "I understand. I'll be back in thirty minutes."

Religion is definitely a factor in my son's marriage. My new daughter-in-law keeps putting burnt offerings on the dinner table, and I keep praying she won't poison him.

Every time we go out to dinner and the check arrives, my son-in-law is a one "I got it" guy. He touches the check and says, "I got it." Then I say, "No, I got it," and he says, "OK."

FIRE
EXTINGUISHER

I could never understand my wife's low threshold of aggravation for her sweet mother until we had our first baby, and Mom and I were alone in our house for three days with only the dog as a buffer.

My daughter-in-law has gone from trying to do her very best to deciding it's enough not to mess up too badly.

My mother-in-law always says, "Don't mind me," so I don't.

The best thing about your son getting married is, when he starts aggravating you, you can send him home to his wife.

MY WIFE COMES FROM A CLOSE, SHARING FAMILY. For fifteen years, my in-laws lived in Ohio and wintered with us in Florida. When my father-in-law died, he was cremated and the urn was left with my brother-in-law in Cleveland.

Months later, as we packed for our vacation, my brother-in-law called and kept my wife, Annette, on the phone. I picked up the extension and inquired, "Annette, do you have our tickets and travelers checks?" Before she could answer he interjected, "Oh yeah, Sis, that reminds me, how would you like to have Dad for the winter?"

CHAPTER 9

AND NOW A WORD FROM OUR SPONSORS

(Advice)

YOU KNOW YOU'RE IN TROUBLE when you know you shouldn't say it and you say it anyway. As one new mother-in-law ruefully put it, "My best talent is advice-giving. I'm good at it. I've been preparing for this role for years. Can I help it if the words just slip out?"

Renowned biblical scholar, Karl Richter notes, "Adam must have been lonely. He had no in-laws at all. The only one who gave advice in Eden was the snake, and look where that got him."

Only much later did helpful in-law advice appear in the "Good Book." Yitro told his son-in-law, Moses, "If you want to make my daughter happy, don't be such a workaholic" (Exodus 18). And after King Saul threw a spear at his son-in-law, David, Saul's son said, "Dad, don't you think you're overreacting?"

(I Samuel Ch 19).

So what chance do we moderns have of dodging unsolicited opinions, when in-law advice carries the weight of historical precedence?

Consider Helen of Troy's mother-in-law, who warned her son, "Menelaus, she's just another pretty face!" Like countless sons before and after him, he shrugged, "Oh, Mom," thereby opening the floodgates of in-law woes for the next ten years. And what about that King Henry VIII? It took six mothers-in-law before he learned, "Henry, it's not good manners to throw your bones on the floor after you've eaten."

Face it, in-laws are always going to give advice. However, whether you follow it or not, well, that's you're choice. After all, Napoleon Bonaparte's father-in-law was the one who said, "What do you mean Emperor of France? Do you really think a little Italian guy from Corsica, who gets his hand caught when he buttons his jacket, will ever amount to anything? Ridiculous!"

When you lend a tool to your brother-in-law, watch him while he uses it and then take it right back.

The secret to being a good father-in-law is, never brag about how much better the other kids are doing.

If you want to make your husband happy, remember his mother's birthday for him.

Nothing ruins a dirty joke quicker than telling it to your mother-in-law.

Good grandparents never tell the grandchildren the whole truth about their parents.

Three things you don't rush . . . sex, marriage and bouillabaisse.

The secret to being a good daughter-in-law is, when you call to talk to "Mom" and your father-in-law says, "I'm sorry, Mom isn't here now," you reply, "Good, that gives me a chance to talk with you."

If your father-in-law is talking to himself, you should have the good sense not to interrupt.

A mother-in-law must listen, swallow, and be quiet.

Never say one of your sons-in-law is better than the other to anyone but your husband—and only when you're sure the house is empty and the radio is turned up loud.

Even if the walls are purple, the floor is green, and the tapwater is brown, tell your married children their first apartment is beautful.

If you want to drive your mother-in-law crazy, monogram every gift you give her. She can't return it and she can't give it to her sister.

Never give advice. Write that on your eyeballs.

The secret to being a good father-in-law is to occasionally give your son-in-law the pleasure of picking up the check.

A good brother-in-law never mentions the skeletons in the closet until after the wedding.

Now that my daughter is dating, my brother-in-law will never let me forget that underneath my three-piece suit lies a '60s flower child in bell-bottom pants with lilacs in my long, stringy beard.

Giving your in-laws a key to your house is certain death.

When Gertrude had her baby, she told her mother-in-law, "I'm worried about my husband's weight, so please watch what he eats

Whenever we travel, my father-in-law wants us to call relatives. When we get back home, he always asks, "By the way, did you call cousin so-and-so?" We always answer truthfully: "We called them but they didn't answer." Because we stand outside the camper and yell, 'Cousin Mabel . . . Cousin Jerome'. . . It's the truth, they never answer.

CAL WARBICK

while I'm in the hospital." For ten days, her mother-in-law cooked all her son's favorites. When a horrified Gertrude saw her husband's expanding waist, her mother-in-law shrugged, "Gertrude, you told me to watch what Aaron eats, and boy, can he eat!"

A good father-in-law lends his kids the down payment for their house; a smart father-in-law makes them sign a note.

If you always do what you always did, you'll always get what you always got.

Early in our marriage, my wife's parents visited us in Michigan. The next morning, Dad said, "David, your sofabed is too valuable to ever sell. It's so damned uncomfortable, no one will ever stay past the first night!" To this day we credit our good family relationships to Dad's advice and our aging "in-law couch."

If your son-in-law is in the room, never talk about him in the "third person invisible."

Never pass up the chance to keep your mouth shut.

The secret to being a good son-in-law is, never tell your in-laws what your parents gave you for your anniversary.

The secret to being a good in-law is, never answer a question that wasn't asked.

The secret to being a good mother-in-law is, keep 'em single.

MY MOTHER-IN-LAW IS EASY TO GET ALONG WITH till you set foot in her kitchen. After being frisked and showing your visa, it's best to sit quietly in the corner. However, one evening after being married to her son for twenty-eight years, I thought it would be safe to volunteer to help with dinner.

Looking distressed, she finally brightened: "All right, dear, I've got just the thing for you to fix." Whereupon she handed me a pot, a measuring cup and a spoon and read me the step-by-step instructions on a box of instant rice.

I guess, except for a few spilled grains on the counter and one leftover serving for which I was held personally responsible, I passed the test, because the next time she let me wash the lettuce.

If you really want to annoy your unmarried brother-in-law, kiss his sister during dinner.

The minute you discover that your husband can—and will—cook and clean, go give your mother-in-law a hug.

If your son-in-law can get it for you wholesale, keep it to yourself.

Being a good mother-in-law means keeping quiet when she feeds your son cold hot dogs and calls it dinner.

A good son-in-law never sits in "Dad's chair."

If you want to annoy your wife, fix up your unmarried brother-in-law with your old girlfriend.

CAL WARBICK

If you'll grant me immunity, I'll talk.

Marsha's fiancé returned to St. Louis for their engagement party. "Mom," said Simon, "you have to help me, because I haven't seen most of our relatives in twenty years." The doorbell rang, the first uncle walked in. Simon whispered, "Mom, help me." "Sure," she replied. "Simon, you remember who this is, don't you?"

CHAPTER 10

SO YOU THOUGHT YOU HAD ALL THE ANSWERS?

PART ONE: AND JUSTICE FOR ALL—

Where Do Your Relatives Land on the In-law/Outlaw Scale?

A Quiz

1. How would you complete the following sentence: "As soon as my in-laws depart after a four-day visit, I . . ."

a. write a thank-you note for the flowers they brought.
b. wipe that smile off my face and let the real me come out.
c. convert the guest room into a bird sanctuary.

2. Does your father-in-law call you

a. son
b. Harry (but my name is Max)
c. as seldom as possible

3. Your spouse's family reunions are

a. a piece of cake
b. a wait-and-see pudding
c. a liver-and-Limburger fricassee

4. Your mother-in-law's favorite drink is

a. a glass of iced tea
b. a demitasse of coffee
c. a pitcher of Zombies

5. Your brother-in-law's favorite quote is

a. "If you cannot get rid of the family skeleton, you may as well make it dance." (George Bernard Shaw)
b. "A good family . . . is one that used to be better." (Cleveland Amory)

c. "I don't have to look up my family tree, because I know that I'm the sap." (Fred Allen)

6. Your sister-in-law reminds you of

a. Mary Tyler Moore
b. Cher
c. Marie Antoinette after the beheading

7. When you take your mother-in-law out to dinner on Mother's Day she says

a. Thank you so much. That was delicious.
b. Don't worry, dear, it's the thought that counts.
c. You call that a restaurant?

8. Your favorite country song is

a. "Let the Good Times Roll"
b. "When They're Old Enough to Know Better, It's Better to Leave Them Alone"
c. "Thank God and Greyhound She's Gone"

9. What is your mother-in-law's philosophy of life?

a. Speak softly but carry a big stick.
b. Sticks and stones may break your bones, but words can never hurt you.
c. If you can't say anything nice about someone, sit next to me.

10. When you sit down for a conversation with your father-in-law, does he

a. lean forward and nod with interest?
b. nod for you to sit back and watch TV wrestling with him?
c. nod off into the popcorn?

11. My father-in-law will never forget

a. our anniversary
b. the incident at our wedding
c. where he buried the hatchet

12. If you found Aladdin's lamp, you'd wish that

a. your best friend had in-laws as nice as yours
b. everyone had in-laws as nice as yours
c. Godzilla had in-laws as nice as yours

Scoring

For question #5, give your in-laws 5 points for each answer.

For all other questions, give your in-laws:

9 points for each (a) answer
5 points for each (b) answer
0 points for each (c) answer.

Results

0-35 points: Count your in-laws among the "Desperados," who often travel in packs and lurk behind every rock in No Man's Land, ready to bushwhack a lone rider. Best to draw your wagons in a circle and call for a posse of friends.

35-80 points: Your "Renegades" are a motley gang, with some real gems salted in among the fool's gold. Keep the genuine sparklers in a nice setting, and bid "vaya con Dios" to the rest as they ride off into the sunset.

80-108 points: If you are lucky enough to have a hacienda full of

"Amigos," count your blessings. Their pictures are tacked up on every fencepost along the Chisholm Trail:

Wanted for: extended families everywhere.

Identifying marks: white hats, generous hearts and buttoned lips.

Last seen: Forging new frontiers with tenderfoot kin, drawing up peace treaties with hostile branches of the clan, and riding herd on family nags before they run roughshod over the old homestead.

Reward: a lifetime of love and laughter.

Part 2: THE IN-LAWFUL OATH OF ALLEGIANCE

I,___________________, do solemnly swear that I will, to the best of my ability, do my duty to preserve, protect and defend ________________, my new ____________-in-law. I will follow that method of treatment which, according to my ability and judgment, I consider to the benefit of my in-laws and will abstain from whatever is deleterious and mischievous. I will not cut my in-law down, but will leave this to be done by other practitioners of this work.

To do this, I will keep myself morally straight, physically strong and mentally awake and will abstain from every voluntary act of mischief.

To maintain the respect due to my ______________-in-law, I will never reject, for a personal consideration, the cause of the defenseless in-law. And from this day forward for better, for worse, for richer, for poorer, in sickness and in health, I will maintain inviolate the confidence to preserve and not spill the beans on this ___________________family secret:________________________
____oops!

If you have funny observations or anecdotes about your own gang of in-laws, please share them with

ALPERN & BLUMENFELD
c/o The In-Law Observation Tower
Box 14413
Atlanta, GA 30324

Photo by Nancy Maxwell Goldberg

ESTHER BLUMENFELD and LYNNE ALPERN began their happy association as a writing team in 1980. Since then they have entertained readers with the best-selling OH LORD, I SOUND JUST LIKE MAMA and MAMA'S COOKING. They appear frequently on radio and TV.

NATIONAL GEOGRAPHIC

ANGRY BIRDS™

FURIOUS FORCES!

v_y

θ

v_x

$\tan\theta = v_y / v_x$

$\theta = \tan^{-1}(v_y / v_x)$

$$0 = -\frac{1}{2}mv^2 + mg(\Delta y)$$

$$v = \sqrt{2g(\Delta y)}$$

$$v = \sqrt{v_x^2 + v_y^2}$$

$$v_2 = \sqrt{\frac{ks^2}{m} - 2gs\sin\theta}$$

$$a_x = 9.8\ m/s^2$$

$$a_x = 0\ m/s^2$$

$$v = 0\ m/s$$

$\vec{F}_{spring}$

s

$\vec{F}_{grav}$

NATIONAL GEOGRAPHIC

ANGRY BIRDS™ FURIOUS FORCES!

The Physics at Play in the World's Most Popular Game

RHETT ALLAIN ★ FOREWORD BY PETER VESTERBACKA

NATIONAL GEOGRAPHIC

Washington, D.C.

Published by the National Geographic Society, 1145 17th Street N.W., Washington, D.C. 20036

Paperback ISBN: 978-1-4262-1172-0
Reinforced library edition ISBN: 978-1-4262-1287-1

CELEBRATING 125 YEARS

The National Geographic Society is one of the world's largest nonprofit scientific and educational organizations. Founded in 1888 to "increase and diffuse geographic knowledge," the Society's mission is to inspire people to care about the planet. It reaches more than 400 million people worldwide each month through its official journal, *National Geographic,* and other magazines; National Geographic Channel; television documentaries; music; radio; films; books; DVDs; maps; exhibitions; live events; school publishing programs; interactive media; and merchandise. National Geographic has funded more than 10,000 scientific research, conservation, and exploration projects and supports an education program promoting geographic literacy.

For more information, visit www.nationalgeographic.com.
National Geographic Society
1145 17th Street N.W.
Washington, D.C. 20036-4688 U.S.A.

For information about special discounts for bulk purchases, please contact
National Geographic Books Special Sales: ngspecsales@ngs.org

For rights or permissions inquiries, please contact National Geographic Books
Subsidiary Rights: ngbookrights@ngs.org

Book design by Jonathan Halling
Printed in United States of America
13/QGT-CML/1

Contents

RESTRICTED AREA
AGITATED
~~AUTHORIZED~~
PERSONNEL ONLY

The Physics of Angry Birds

Angry Birds fans come face-to-face with basic principles of physics every time they take aim with the slingshot. At what angle should an Angry Bird be launched for it to hit the target and to knock out as many pigs as possible with one shot? How should acceleration and mass be taken into account in the pig hunt? How does gravity affect the flight of the Angry Birds?

National Geographic has taken on the task to explain the apparent connection between the Angry Birds game and physics as a science. Both focus on achieving the optimal result or finding a solution by trial and error. Angry Birds and physics are a natural match because, in the end, both are characterized by immersion, exploration, and even playfulness. This book has been born out of the inspiring collaboration between Rovio and National Geographic.

Physics can be fun, just like playing Angry Birds!

Peter Vesterbacka
Mighty Eagle & CMO
Rovio Entertainment Ltd.

LEVEL 1 MECHANICS

A branch of physical science that deals with energy and forces and their effect on bodies

A skydiver, while being influenced by gravity and the air, falls toward the Earth.

PHYSICS AT PLAY

IN 350 B.C., ARISTOTLE WAS ONE OF THE FIRST TO STUDY MOTION. TOO BAD HE WAS MOSTLY WRONG.

DESCRIBING MOTION

If you want to talk about what a force does to an object, you need a way to describe the object's motion. Just how do you do that? I could describe their motion by drawing a picture of the path—or *trajectory*—the object took. Of course, you have already seen trajectories. When you launch an Angry Bird at a pig, you see the path the bird traveled.

Although a trajectory can be very useful, it still doesn't tell the whole story. It doesn't say anything about the how fast the object moves. Often we will use a mathematical expression to describe the motion of an object. Unsurprisingly, this is called the equation of motion.

INTERACTIONS & FORCE

Physics isn't just about forces; it really looks at interactions. What's an interaction? You could say that any time two objects influence each other, that is an interaction. Think of an Angry Bird hitting a block. Both the block and the bird change in some manner, so we say there was an interaction. It turns out that the idea of force is just a way to describe interactions.

What exactly is a force? You have felt forces yourself. Place a book in your hand. It pushes down on you, and you can feel that. That is a force. When a slingshot pulls on an Angry Bird, that's a force, too. In this level, we are going to look at what forces do to objects.

There are two common units used when measuring forces: the newton and the pound. A typical hardbound book might weigh around 10 newtons, which is a little over 2 pounds.

ARISTOTLE'S & NEWTON'S IDEAS ABOUT FORCE

Now let's put these two ideas together: What happens to an object that has a constant force on it? This is a very old question. No one really knows the first person, or group of people, to explore these concepts, but we often credit the ancient Greek philosopher Aristotle with many of the original ideas. Unfortunately, Aristotle wasn't really a scientist, and although he was a great thinker, he never backed up his ideas with experimental evidence. For Aristotle, keeping a constant force on an object would make it move at a constant speed. Although this seems to make sense, it's just not true. It wasn't until about 2,000 years after Aristotle that Sir Isaac Newton and Galileo Galilei explored the effects of force. They found that with a constant force, you actually get a constant *change* in motion. If there is no force, the motion doesn't change at all.

LOOK AT THAT KINETIC ENERGY AT WORK!

DESCRIBING ANGRY BIRDS' MOTION WITH ENERGY

Forces aren't the only game in town when it comes to describing interactions. There is another viewpoint that we can use: energy. We can look at any interaction and describe it either in terms of forces or by using the idea of energy.

Even though we use energy so often in our everyday lives, it is surprisingly difficult to define. Perhaps the best way to understand energy is to look at some examples. A moving Angry Bird has a type of energy that we call *kinetic energy.* The faster a bird moves, the more energy it has.

But where did this energy come from? It might come from the energy stored in the rubber band of the slingshot that the bird was launched from. And where does this kinetic energy go? As the bird gets higher, it slows down, so its kinetic energy decreases. In order for the total energy to remain constant, some other type of energy has to increase. We call this energy associated with objects moving up or down the *gravitational potential energy.*

MOTION

Did you see that car zoom by? If you did, how would you describe its motion? Well, I just described it—I said "zoom." This may be a colorful way to talk about the motion of the car, but it isn't very useful. Cars can move in all sorts of ways, and we need to describe their motion with a little more detail.

WHAT ARE POSITION, VELOCITY, AND ACCELERATION?

Here we have a car in a race. How can we describe the motion of this car? First, we establish a *position,* which is the distance the car is from some particular spot, such as the starting line. When it comes to motion, we are most interested in the *displacement* of the object—the distance the car moves from one time and location to another time and location. Essentially, it's not where you are that's important, it's your change in location.

If we look at the displacement of the car and divide that by how long it took to travel this distance, we get the *velocity,* or how fast the car is moving. The velocity tells us how the position changes with time, and the *acceleration* tells us how the velocity changes with time.

PHYSI-FACTS

WE CAN MEASURE POSITION AND DISPLACEMENT IN INCHES, FEET, OR METERS, AMONG OTHER UNITS.

VELOCITY CAN BE MEASURED IN UNITS OF MILES PER HOUR (MPH), FEET PER SECOND, OR METERS PER SECOND.

ACCELERATION CAN BE MEASURED IN MPH PER SECOND, FEET PER SECOND PER SECOND, OR METERS PER SECOND PER SECOND.

A rally car is briefly airborne during a race. Zoom.

FORCES & MOTION

What happens if you use your hand to push on a baseball, like a pitcher does when he throws? Since the ball starts at rest, this force changes the velocity of the ball from zero to a nonzero value—perhaps more than 90 mph, if you are a professional.

WHAT DOES FORCE DO TO AN OBJECT?

What happens after you let go of the baseball? You're no longer pushing on the ball, because you're not touching it. If there aren't any other forces on the ball—such as a bat hitting the ball—the ball shouldn't change its velocity. Actually, there *are* other forces, like gravity and air resistance, interacting with the ball, but over the short time from the pitcher's mound to home plate, these forces don't have much impact on the velocity.

Forces can make an object speed up or slow down. When the ball interacts with the catcher's glove, the catcher pushes on the ball in a direction opposite to its velocity. This causes the velocity to decrease quickly to zero. In either instance, forces change the velocity. If there is no force, there is no change.

PHYSICS AT PLAY

PLACE A BALL ON A SMOOTH SURFACE. WHEN YOU TAP ON THE BALL, IT WILL CHANGE ITS VELOCITY. TAP IN THE SAME DIRECTION AS ITS MOTION AND IT WILL SPEED UP. TAP IN THE OPPOSITE DIRECTION AND IT WILL SLOW DOWN.

The baseball's motion is caused by the force from the pitcher.

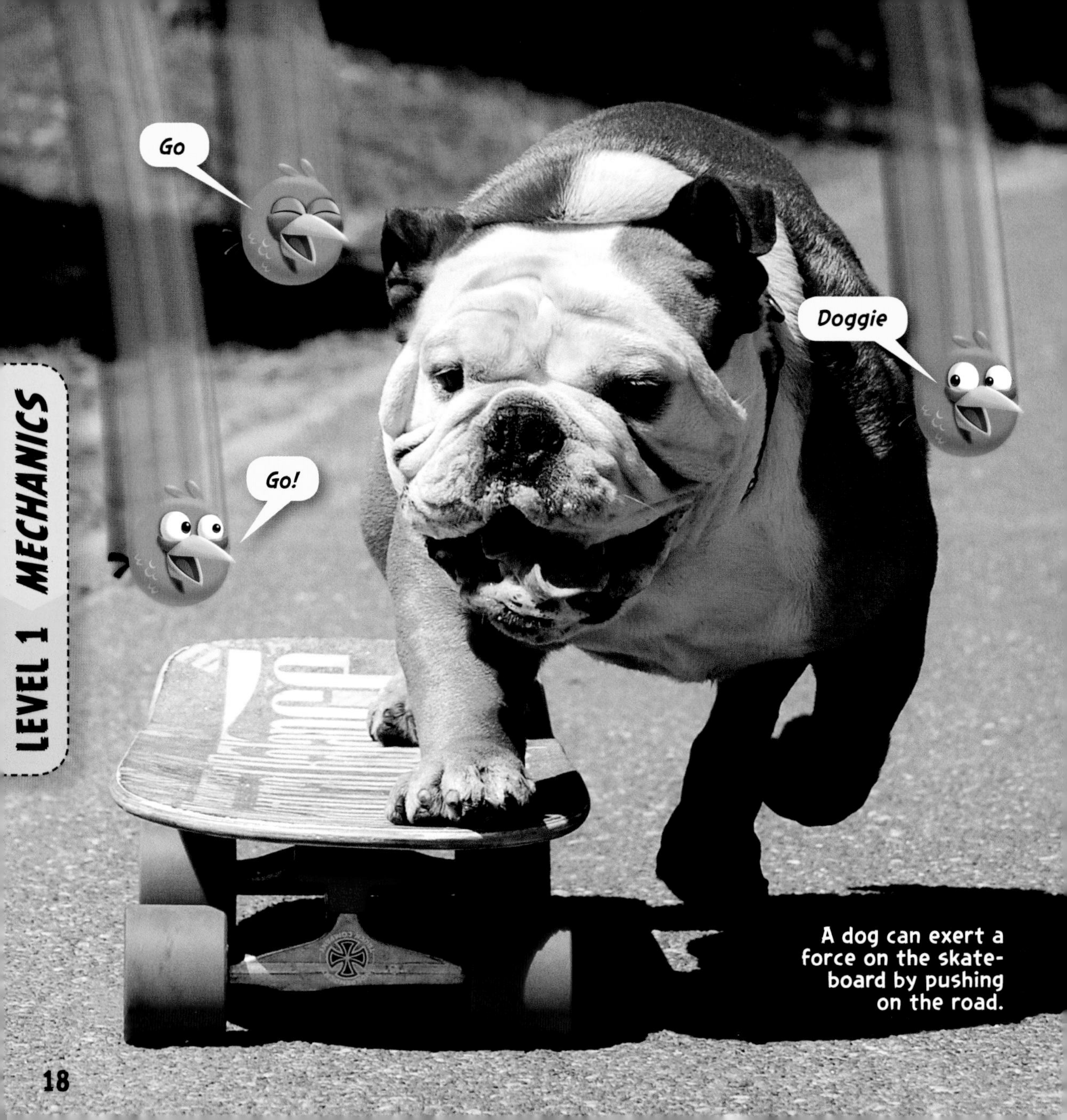

A dog can exert a force on the skate-board by pushing on the road.

CONSTANT FORCES

Why would a dog ride a skateboard? Better yet, why don't *all* dogs ride skateboards? The nice thing about skateboards is that they have very little friction. If the dog gets on the board with a push, she will move at a fairly constant speed. But what if she continues to push as she rides on the board? We already know that a force changes the velocity of an object. So, if you constantly have a force on the object, its velocity will constantly change. The dog on a skateboard would just keep speeding up.

WHAT HAPPENS IF A CONSTANT FORCE KEEPS ACTING ON AN OBJECT?

Now, what if I push on an object with a greater constant force? Does this make the object just go faster? Not exactly. Remember that constant forces continually change the velocity, so even a tiny force can eventually result in a very large speed. A greater force simply means that the velocity will change much more quickly.

PHYSI-FACTS

THE CONVERSION FOR UNITS OF FORCE IS 1 NEWTON = 0.22 POUNDS OR 1 POUND = 4.45 NEWTONS.

THE POUND IS OFTEN USED AS A UNIT OF MASS, BUT IT IS ACTUALLY A UNIT OF FORCE.

THE ENGLISH UNIT FOR MASS IS THE SLUG, AND THE METRIC UNIT FOR MASS IS THE KILOGRAM.

THE SATURN V ROCKET CAN EXERT A THRUST FORCE OF UP TO 34 MILLION NEWTONS (7.5 MILLION POUNDS).

GRAVITY

Gravity is the one force that we all experience. The gravitational force is an interaction between all objects with mass. However, for most objects, this interaction is much too small to notice. On Earth, when we talk about gravity, we are probably talking about the gravitational pull of the Earth.

WHY DOES A BALL SLOW DOWN AFTER YOU THROW IT IN THE AIR?

What happens if you take a cup and let go? Once you let go, there is only the constant gravitational force pulling down on the cup. A constant force means a constantly changing velocity. The cup will continue to speed up as it falls until some other force acts on it. Unfortunately, this other force is probably going to be from the ground pushing up on the cup and causing it to break.

What if you threw a cup, or a ball, up in the air? Gravity still pulls down on it. But in this case the force is in the opposite direction to the velocity, which means the cup will slow down as it rises until it stops. After that, it will fall back down and increase in velocity.

PHYSICS AT PLAY

START UP THE ANGRY BIRDS GAME. INSTEAD OF LAUNCHING A BIRD AT THE PIGS, TRY SOMETHING DIFFERENT. LAUNCH THE BIRD ALMOST STRAIGHT UP. THE GRAVITATIONAL FORCE PULLS DOWN ON THE BIRD, AND THIS MAKES IT SLOW DOWN.

If you don't exert forces on objects, gravity will cause them to fall, like this glass of milk.

RED

MAN ON A MISSION

Red's mechanics aren't rocket science; determination to protect the eggs drives him in the right direction. Their safety is no small responsibility, and Red fancies himself the leader of the whole Angry Birds flock. Velocity is his greatest weapon, as he takes off in pursuit of those pesky, egg-snatching pigs. The more furious Red gets, the more motivated he is to move, fearlessly hurtling himself toward the enemy. This fed-up flyer proves that standing sentry is one thing, but the best watch guards know when to get going.

ISAAC NEWTON

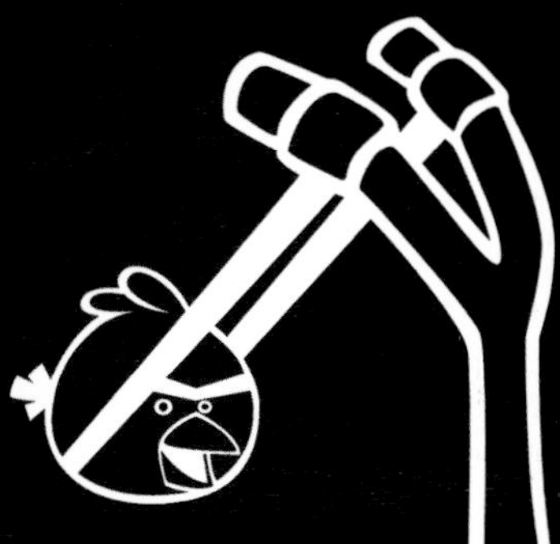

$$v = (x_2 - x_1)/t$$

NAME: RED

WHAT MAKES RED MOVE: HIS TRUSTY SLINGSHOT

FAVORITE TACTIC: DIRECT HIT ON THE TARGET

PHYSICS AT PLAY: VELOCITY TELLS US HOW LONG IT TAKES TO MOVE A CERTAIN DISTANCE.

TERMINAL VELOCITY

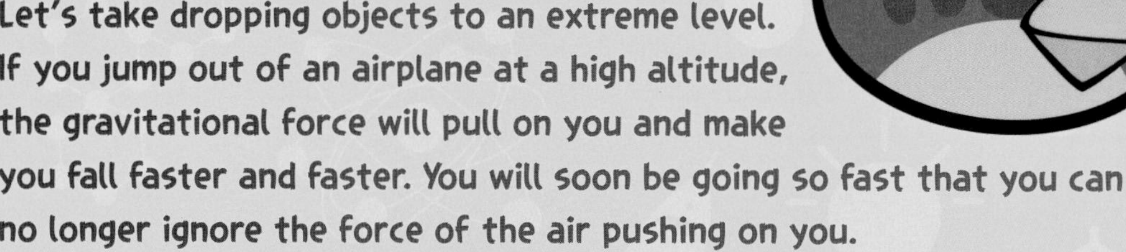

Let's take dropping objects to an extreme level. If you jump out of an airplane at a high altitude, the gravitational force will pull on you and make you fall faster and faster. You will soon be going so fast that you can no longer ignore the force of the air pushing on you.

WHY DOESN'T A SKYDIVER KEEP INCREASING IN SPEED?

You can easily feel air resistance force by holding your hand out of a car window. The faster you go, the more the air pushes against your hand. This is what happens to a skydiver. The faster he falls, the greater the air resistance's force. Eventually, the air resistance force will have the same value as the gravitational force, but in the opposite direction. These two forces acting together are exactly the same as if no force was acting on the jumper, so the person will move at a constant velocity. We call this *terminal velocity,* since it is the end of increasing speed.

PHYSI-FACTS

A TYPICAL SKYDIVER HAS A TERMINAL SPEED OF 54 METERS PER SECOND (120 MPH).

A SKYDIVER CAN CHANGE HER TERMINAL SPEED BY CHANGING HER BODY POSITION AND THUS THE AREA IN CONTACT WITH THE AIR.

Skydivers in free fall can arrange themselves in different formations.

PROJECTILE MOTION

If you want an arrow to hit a target, you have to give some thought to physics. After the arrow leaves the bow, there is essentially just one force acting on it: gravity. Since the gravitational force only pulls down, it changes the velocity only in the vertical direction. The horizontal velocity doesn't change.

HOW DO YOU SHOOT AN ARROW FARTHER?

An arrow shot horizontally won't go as far as an arrow shot at a slight upward angle. Why? The inclined arrow has some initial velocity in the vertical direction. This means that it will take longer for the arrow to start moving down toward the ground. The longer time gives the arrow more time to travel horizontally. If you aim *too* high, you decrease the horizontal velocity a lot.

PHYSICS AT PLAY

YOU CAN TRY PROJECTILE MOTION IN THE ANGRY BIRDS GAME. PICK A LEVEL AND LAUNCH THE BIRD HORIZONTALLY. HOW FAR DID IT GO? NOW LAUNCH AT A SLIGHTLY INCLINED ANGLE. DOES IT GO FARTHER?

Once an arrow leaves the bow, its motion is determined by gravity.

GRAVITY & WEIGHT

You have undoubtedly been in an elevator as it travels to a higher floor. By doing this, the elevator accelerates upward to obtain a nonzero velocity. What does it feel like to be in the elevator? You feel slightly heavier when the elevator accelerates upward, and you feel slightly lighter when the elevator stops, accelerating in a downward direction.

WHY DO YOU FEEL HEAVIER OR LIGHTER IN AN ELEVATOR?

Are you actually getting lighter? No. Remember that the gravitational force depends on the masses of the two objects interacting. Neither the Earth nor your mass changes in an elevator. So what is going on? The short answer is that what we feel as our weight isn't actually our weight. Instead, we feel the other forces pushing on us. When accelerating upward in an elevator, the floor has to push with a greater force than gravity to get you to accelerate. Since this force is greater than your weight, you feel heavier. The reverse happens when you accelerate downward in an elevator. The floor doesn't need to push as hard as gravity, so you feel lighter.

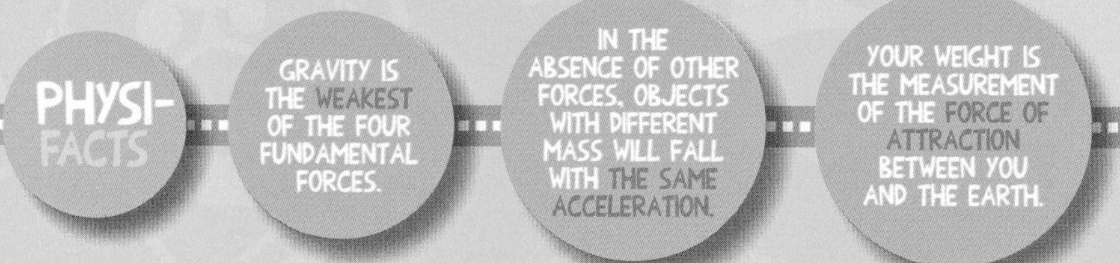

If you were on an accelerating rocket, would you feel different?

KING PIG

SIZE DOES MATTER

If mass is related to rate of motion, it's going to take serious force to make King Pig step aside. This stationary swine is the mastermind behind stealing the Angry Birds' eggs, and he's keen to fill his cooking pot without lifting a finger. He inertly sits and waits as his minions hunt, hoping they'll outsmart enough Angry Birds to satisfy his hunger. Piggy Island has long been his playpen, but he ventures from his throne only when provoked—or pummeled—into action. Even then, his rotund roll is no match for the Angry Birds' feathered fury.

GALILEO GALILEI

$$F_{\{net\}} = ma$$

NAME: KING PIG

WHAT MAKES KING PIG MOVE: THE WRATHFUL FORCE OF AN ANGRY BIRD

FAVORITE TACTIC: STANDING HIS GROUND

PHYSICS AT PLAY: THE LAW OF INERTIA STATES THAT AN OBJECT AT REST WILL REMAIN AT REST UNTIL ACTED ON BY AN OUTSIDE FORCE.

ASTRONAUTS IN ORBIT

The common idea is that there is no gravity in space. This causes astronauts to appear weightless. But there is indeed gravity in space—in fact, the Earth orbits the sun only because of a gravitational interaction.

WHY DO ASTRONAUTS FLOAT IN SPACE?

The farther you get from the Earth, the weaker the gravitational force gets. However, astronauts in orbit are only 300 kilometers (185 miles) above the Earth, which has a diameter of almost 13,000 kilometers (8,000 miles). This makes the gravitational force in orbit only slightly smaller than on Earth. Then why are they weightless?

It turns out that the space station is like the accelerating elevator we talked about. The only difference is that it is always accelerating. Since both the "elevator" and the astronaut are accelerating as they move around the Earth, there is no force needed to push on the astronaut other than gravity. No other force means that the astronaut feels weightless.

PHYSICS AT PLAY

IN ORBIT AT THE LEVEL OF THE INTERNATIONAL SPACE STATION, THE GRAVITATIONAL FORCE IS ABOUT 90 PERCENT OF THE VALUE AT THE SURFACE OF THE EARTH.

An astronaut on a space walk outside the space shuttle.

ENERGY & MOTION

The path of a roller coaster can be crazy. You may have noticed that as the car on the track goes up and down, it speeds up and slows down. Can this motion be described using the terms of energy instead of forces? Yes, and in many ways it is easier to describe. For a twisting track, it can be quite difficult to keep up with the different forces acting on the car. With an energy approach, we can just look at where the car started and where it stopped.

A roller coaster is fun because it speeds up and slows down.

CAN WE USE ENERGY TO DESCRIBE A ROLLER COASTER?

For a roller coaster, there are really two important types of energy. There is kinetic energy, the energy associated with the motion of the car. This depends on both the mass of the car and the velocity. The other energy is the gravitational potential energy, the energy associated with the gravitational interaction between the Earth and the car. Potential energy depends on the mass of the car and its height above the surface of the Earth.

In the case of a roller coaster on a track, there are no energy inputs into the system. This means that the sum of kinetic and potential energy must be a constant. As the car goes downward, potential energy decreases, so the kinetic energy must increase, which makes the car go faster.

CIRCULAR MOTION

We've talked about acceleration, but there is more to that story. Velocity is really a quantity that takes into account both how fast something is moving and in what direction. It's what we call a *vector.* Changing any part of this vector is acceleration. Even at a constant speed, moving in a circle is acceleration.

WHY DO WET MAMMALS SHAKE TO DRY OFF?

Getting dry seems to be all about the acceleration of the water. A shaking mammal essentially moves its fur back and forth in a circular motion. The faster something moves in a circle, the greater the acceleration that water would have. How do you get something to accelerate? Remember from before, we established that you need a force to accelerate this water. For water on fur, there is a type of frictional force that can keep the water moving in a circle. Of course, if you spin fast enough, this frictional force will not be enough to keep the water moving in a circle and it will fly off. Then you have a dry and happy mammal. Everyone is happier when they are dry—well, except for fish.

PHYSI-FACTS

FOR AN OBJECT MOVING IN A CIRCLE, THE ACCELERATION IS DIRECTED TOWARD THE CENTER OF THE CIRCLE.

THE VALUE OF THE CIRCULAR ACCELERATION INCREASES WITH THE SPEED OF THE OBJECT, BUT DECREASES AS THE RADIUS OF THE CIRCULAR MOTION GETS BIGGER.

A polar bear dries its fur by shaking in a circular motion.

LEVEL 2 SOUND & LIGHT

Traveling vibrations that extend out from an oscillating source: sound through a material medium, light in both electric and magnetic fields

This classic image incorrectly portrays sound as windlike.

OSCILLATING MASS

If you take a spring (or a rubber band, if you don't have a spring) and pull it, the spring pulls back. If you squeeze a spring, it will push back the other way. If you take a small weight, like a rock, and hang it on a spring, the rock will just hang there motionless. The spring, though, is pulling up on the rock with the same force that gravity pulls down. Now, what if you pull the rock down a little bit? The stretched spring will exert a force on the rock that is greater than the rock's gravitational force. When you let go, the rock will start to move up. But it won't continue to move up forever—it will soon get to a point where it goes back down. We call this back-and-forth motion an *oscillation,* which is important to our understanding of light.

DESCRIBING WAVES

When we talk about waves, we usually have an image in our mind of waves that repeat on a regular pattern, such as waves in the ocean. In a wave, there isn't just one displacement that moves, but many.

We can describe these repeating waves with three measurements. The first is the *wave speed.* If you tracked just one wave in the ocean and measured its speed from point A to point B, that would be the wave speed. The second is the *wave frequency.* Suppose you were sitting on a rock sticking out of the water. If you counted how many waves went past the rock every second, that would be the frequency. The third measurement is the *wavelength.* The wavelength is the distance from the crest of one wave to the crest of the next wave. Yes, even if it is a sound wave or a wave on a Slinky, you can measure wave speed, wave frequency, and wavelength.

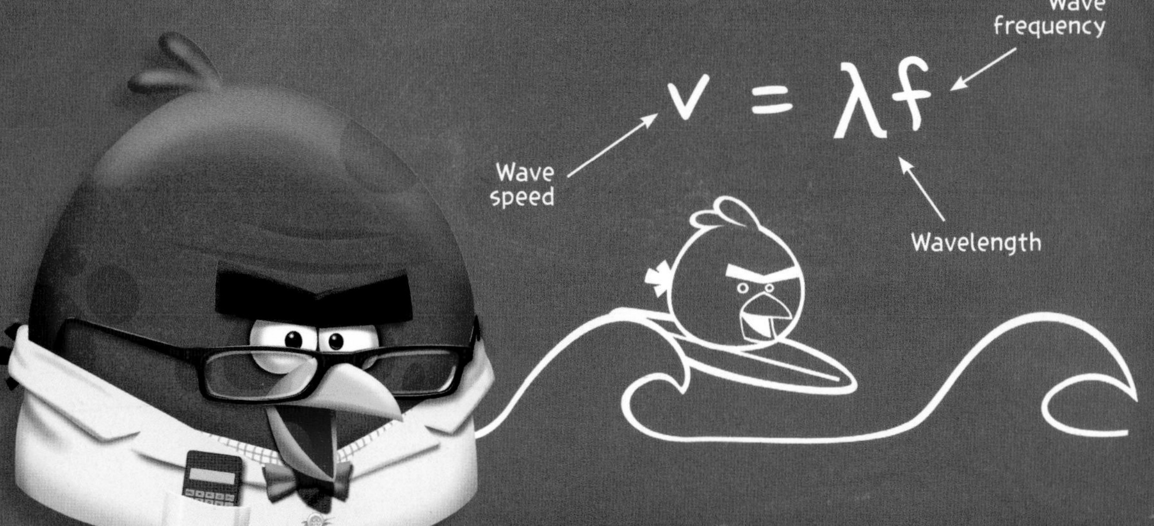

WHAT IS SOUND?

Suppose you take your hand and shake it back and forth. When you do this, you push the air (unless you are an astronaut in space or a mermaid). Even though air is thin, it runs into some more air, and in turn pushes it forward. The result is a compression wave of air molecules.

Now suppose you could move your hand back and forth 200 times every second. If you could do this, the compression air waves you would be creating would be heard by other people's ears. Well, you can't do it with your hand, but you *can* do it with your vocal cords or a rubber band or a tuning fork. All of these are able to vibrate really fast, which creates sound waves.

Since sound is a wave, we know it has a wave speed, a wavelength, and a frequency. If you increase the frequency, the human ear interprets this as a higher pitch sound.

WHO KNEW SOUND AND LIGHT WERE SIMILAR?

WHAT IS LIGHT?

Sound is a wave, and so is light, but light is very different. Imagine what would happen if you removed the air from a room. How would sound travel through air that's not there? It couldn't.

Now, what about light? Sound travels through air and ocean waves travel through water, so if light is a wave, what does it travel through? The answer is a little tricky. It doesn't travel through anything—because light is a wave in itself. Crazy, I know. We call light an *electromagnetic wave.* It consists of oscillations in an electric field along with oscillations in a magnetic field. Together, these two fields allow the light to travel through "empty" space. That's how light gets from the sun to us and the green growing plants.

WAVES

You can create waves at home. Take a long string and lay it on the ground in a straight line. Now grab one end and give it a quick shake. What happens next? You will see a nice wave travel down the string. Look closely at the string and you'll see the string also moves side to side, making a wave that travels down the string. Therefore, you can see that a wave is a traveling displacement.

HOW CAN PEOPLE MAKE A WAVE?

You've probably participated in a "wave" of fans at a sporting event. Essentially, the same thing happens in a people wave as the wave on a string—the people move up and down, and the wave moves around the stadium. The key idea is that the people are not moving all the way around the stadium themselves; instead, it is the *disturbance* of the people that moves.

It doesn't matter what kind of wave we are talking about: people, string, sound, light. In all of these waves, it is the disturbance that moves.

PHYSICS AT PLAY

A PEOPLE WAVE CAN TRAVEL ALL THE WAY AROUND AN AVERAGE-SIZE STADIUM IN UNDER 30 SECONDS, REACHING A SPEED OF 55 MILES AN HOUR (25 M/S). IT WOULD TAKE A PERSON RUNNING AT FULL SPEED TWICE THE AMOUNT OF TIME TO GO THE SAME DISTANCE.

A ribbon in rhythmic gymnastics can carry a wave as part of a routine.

THUNDER &

Have you ever heard someone counting the time between a flash of lightning and the sound of thunder? They do this to get an estimate of the distance from a storm, but how does it work?

Both the sound from thunder and the flash from lightning are types of waves. Thunder is a sound wave, and light is an electromagnetic wave. Both waves are created at essentially the same instant in time, but these kinds of waves have different speeds. If you are 10 miles from a lightning strike, the light gets there almost instantly. However, it takes the sound from the thunder almost a minute to get to you. The closer you are to the lightning strike, the quicker you hear the boom.

HOW DO YOU CALCULATE THE DISTANCE YOU ARE FROM A LIGHTNING STRIKE?

OK, flash! You see a flash of light from lightning. 1, 2, 3, 4, 5 . . . 10. You get to ten seconds and then—BOOM!—hear the thunder. Since sound travels 1 mile in 5 seconds, this means that the lightning was 2 miles away.

Lightning strikes a tower in Toronto.

LIGHTNING

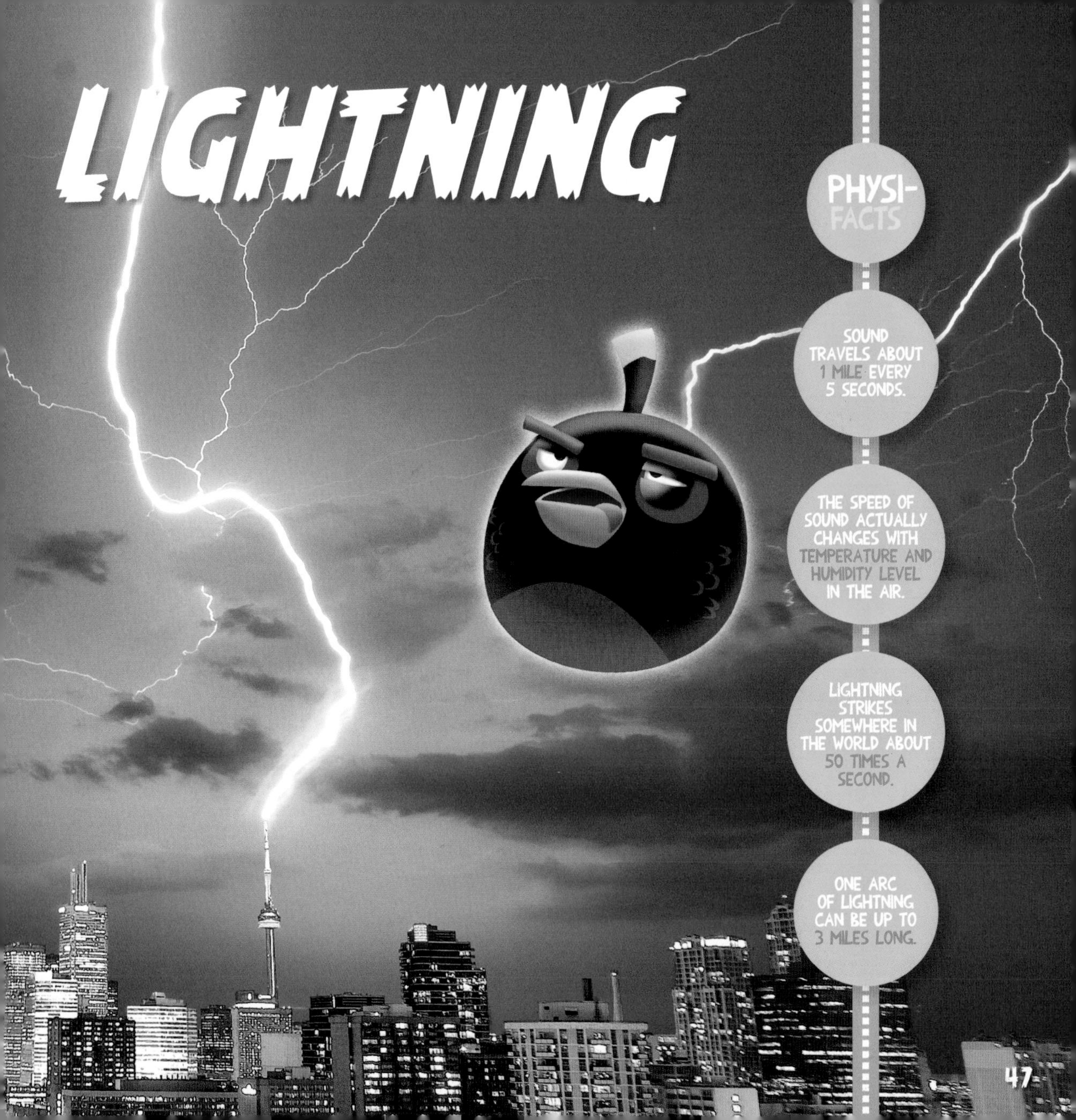

PHYSI-FACTS

SOUND TRAVELS ABOUT 1 MILE EVERY 5 SECONDS.

THE SPEED OF SOUND ACTUALLY CHANGES WITH TEMPERATURE AND HUMIDITY LEVEL IN THE AIR.

LIGHTNING STRIKES SOMEWHERE IN THE WORLD ABOUT 50 TIMES A SECOND.

ONE ARC OF LIGHTNING CAN BE UP TO 3 MILES LONG.

Sound waves can travel through the air or a string.

STANDING WAVES

What happens when a wave comes to the end of the material that it is moving through? In the case of a wave on a string, it will bounce back. This is what happens when you pluck a guitar string. If this is a repeating wave, one wave will be reflecting back while another one is still traveling in the original direction. There will be two waves on the string moving in different directions.

WHAT HAPPENS WHEN TWO WAVES TRY TO SHARE A STRING?

The two waves traveling on the same string can either reduce or reinforce each other. If one wave has an upward displacement and the other has an equal downward displacement, they will cancel one another. If both waves have displacements in the same direction, these displacements add together to make a bigger wave. This is called a standing wave. With a guitar string, only certain wavelengths can travel back and forth without destroying the reflected waves. It is because of this that a plucked guitar string makes such a pleasant sound.

PHYSICS AT PLAY

YOU CAN SEE WAVE MOTION USING A JUMP ROPE. FIND A PARTNER AND A LONG JUMP ROPE. HAVE YOUR PARTNER HOLD ONE END STEADY, WHILE YOU CREATE WAVES BY SHAKING THE ROPE UP AND DOWN. HAVE A PARTNER TRY ADDING IN A SMALLER WAVE FROM THE OTHER END.

CHUCK

READY, SET . . . JET

Always ready to strike, Chuck moves at lightning speed and he's a bird on a mission. Chuck is Red's self-proclaimed second in command, eager to prove his worth. Some call him hyperactive, but his avian brethren rely on his supersonic service to defend their noble cause. With the constant threat of scheming piggies—as well as feathered rivals competing for his sidekick role—Chuck knows he has to stay on his talons.

CHARLES "CHUCK" YEAGER

Mach 1 = 340.29 m/s

NAME: CHUCK

WHAT MAKES CHUCK MOVE: ANYTHING THAT THREATENS HIS SUPERIORITY

FAVORITE TACTIC: TRY, TRY AGAIN FASTER

PHYSICS AT PLAY: THE MACH NUMBER IS THE SPEED OF AN OBJECT DIVIDED BY THE SPEED OF SOUND IN THE SAME FLUID MEDIUM (GAS OR LIQUID).

LEVEL 2
SOUND & LIGHT

SOUND IN SOLIDS & LIQUIDS

Have ever been underwater in a pool? Sometimes you can hear noises underwater, but it is very difficult to determine where those noises come from. Out of the water, your brain can get a much better idea of the location of sounds. Since sound takes time to travel, one ear might actually hear a noise before the other ear. This means a small time difference between ears making it difficult to determine direction.

HOW DO DOLPHINS NAVIGATE IN MURKY WATER?

Some animals actually rely on sound to help them get a bearing on their surroundings. Dolphins create high-pitched squeaks in order to find food and navigate. These squeaks travel through the water and bounce off anything solid, like fish and obstacles. The longer it takes for the sound to get back to the dolphin, the farther away the object is. We know this process as *echolocation.*

PHYSI-FACTS

- SOUND TRAVELS TWO AND A HALF TIMES FASTER IN WATER THAN IN AIR.
- SUBMARINES USE A SIMILAR TECHNIQUE TO DOLPHINS CALLED ACTIVE SONAR.
- THE FIRST PATENT FOR AN UNDERWATER SONAR DEVICE WAS FILED IN 1912.
- THE SOUNDS FROM A HUMPBACK WHALE CAN TRAVEL HUNDREDS OF MILES.

DOPPLER EFFECT

We know that sound is a wave and therefore has a wavelength. Higher pitched sounds have a shorter wavelength than lower pitched sounds. But something interesting happens if the source of sound is moving.

A motorcycle sounds different coming and going.

VVVVVVVVRRRRRRRRRO

WHY DOES THE PITCH OF A MOTORCYCLE'S ENGINE CHANGE AS IT MOVES PAST YOU?

Imagine a motorcycle roaring past you from left to right at some constant speed. The engine creates one sound wave, and then the motorcycle moves closer to you before the engine makes the next one. This creates the appearance of a smaller wavelength compared to a stationary motorcycle, called the *Doppler shift.* As the motorcycle approaches, the sound from its engine has a Doppler shift to give it a higher pitch; when it is driving away from you, the pitch sounds lower. The faster the motorcycle moves, the greater the Doppler shift. This Doppler effect can happen for any type of wave produced from a moving source.

PHYSICS AT PLAY

DOPPLER RADAR, USED BY WEATHER STATIONS, LOOKS AT THE CHANGE IN FREQUENCY OF RADAR WAVES AS THEY BOUNCE OFF WEATHER SYSTEMS. BY LOOKING AT THE CHANGE IN FREQUENCY, THE SYSTEM CAN DETERMINE IF A WEATHER SYSTEM IS MOVING TOWARD OR AWAY FROM THE DETECTOR.

OOOOOOOOOOMMMMMMM

SEEING IN THE DARK

What happens when you are in a dark room? Usually your eyes adjust to the minimal light, and you can see. If it were absolutely dark, you would see absolutely nothing. But it is rarely completely dark. In your room, you probably have some tiny lights on your clock. With even a little bit of light, we can see. Even the stars in the night sky coming through a

PHYSI-FACTS

THE UNIT OF MEASUREMENT FOR THE BRIGHTNESS OF A LIGHT SOURCE IS THE CANDELA (CD).

window can let enough light into your room so that it isn't completely dark. In order to see anything, light has to reflect off of an object and travel to your eyes. If there is no light, there is no seeing.

HOW DO ANIMALS SEE IN THE DARK?

Night-dwelling animals usually have big eyes. With larger eyes, they can gather more of the low levels of light to get a view of what is around. What about bats in a cave? Caves are one of the few places you can get that have essentially no light at all. Bats get around this problem by using echolocation just like dolphins.

What do you see in absolute darkness? Black.

OWLS CAN SEE **35 TO 100 TIMES BETTER** IN LOW LIGHT THAN HUMANS.

A SMALL CANDLE EMITS LIGHT WITH THE **LUMINOSITY** OF ROUGHLY ONE CANDELA.

INFRARED LIGHT

Maybe I didn't tell the whole truth before. I said that in order for us to see something, light has to reflect off of it. Well, what about a lightbulb? Light doesn't reflect off that. Instead it makes its own light. It turns out that all objects emit light. Yes, even *you* emit light. However, this light isn't always light that we can see. If the wavelength is longer than the color red, our eyes can't detect it; we call this light *infrared.* Yet, even though you can't see it, you can detect it with a special camera.

WHAT'S SO SPECIAL ABOUT INFRARED LIGHT?

The color of light an object emits depends on its temperature. For most objects we see (with reflected light), the light they emit is in the infrared region. So, measuring the infrared light from something can tell us its temperature. This is how those in-ear thermometers work.

If an object gets really hot, the light it gives off moves into the visible range, beginning with the color red. This is where the term "red hot" comes from. If you keep increasing the temperature of something, it will start to appear white or blue.

PHYSI-FACTS

TV REMOTE CONTROLS USE SHORT, NEAR-INFRARED WAVES.

SOME FAST-FOOD RESTAURANTS USE LAMPS THAT EMIT INFRARED LIGHT TO KEEP FOOD WARM.

SNAKES IN THE PIT VIPER FAMILY HAVE THE ABILITY TO IMAGE INFRARED LIGHT TO CATCH WARM-BLOODED PREY.

HUMANS RADIATE INFRARED LIGHT AT A WAVELENGTH OF ABOUT 10 MICRONS.

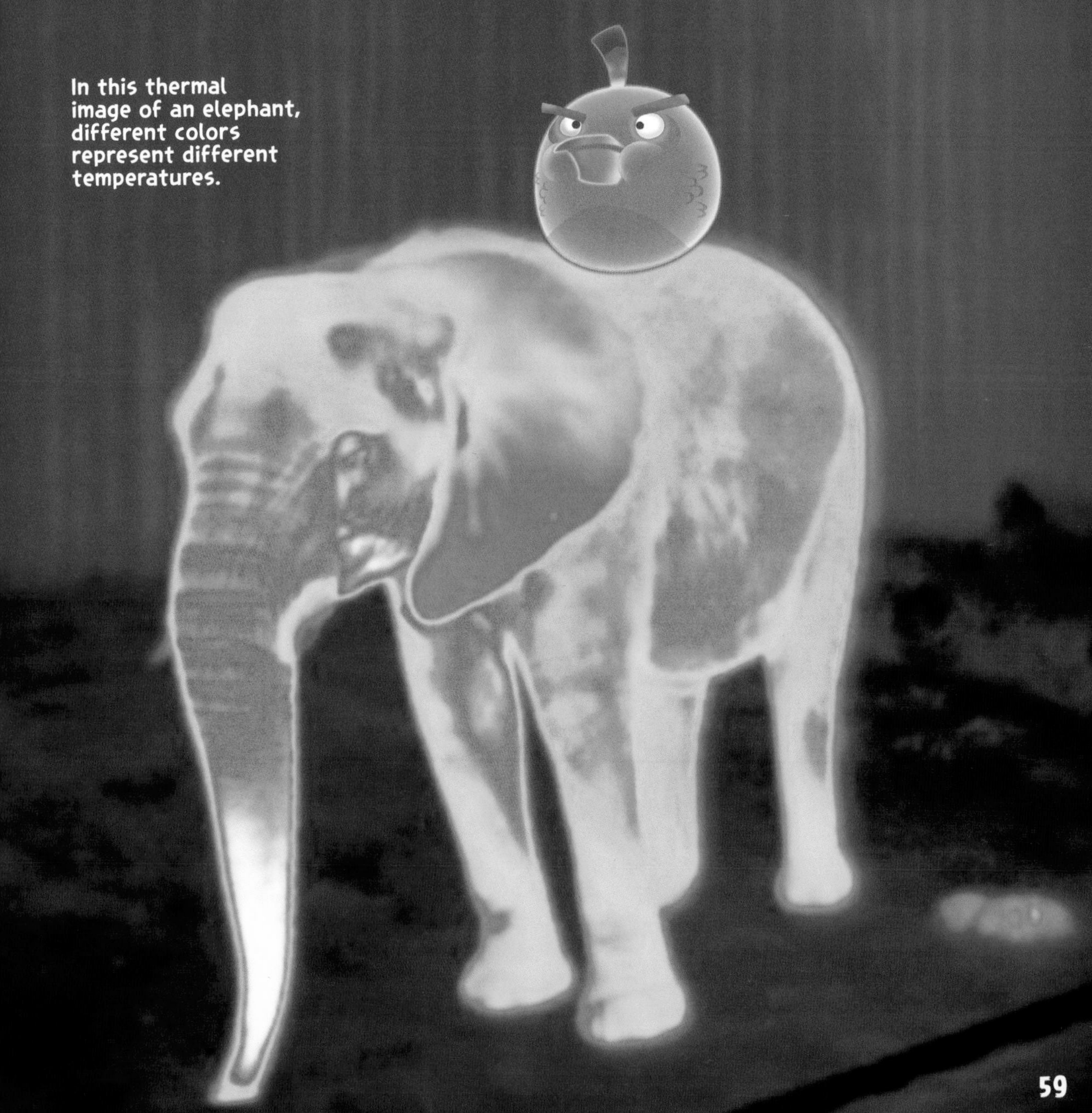

In this thermal image of an elephant, different colors represent different temperatures.

MATILDA

AURA BEFORE ANGER

Peace, love, and free-range earthworms are all Matilda needs to sing her happy tune. It takes a lot to ruffle her pure white feathers, but wasteful piggies really get her riled up. Though she is hopeful for harmony, she's been known to get aggressive when the occasion calls for it. Matilda's in awe of all things shiny, believing that light waves give her special energy. She draws inspiration from each brilliant ray and its refractive powers, illuminating the forest from every angle.

ALHAZEN

$$n_1 \sin\theta_1 = n_2 \sin\theta_2$$

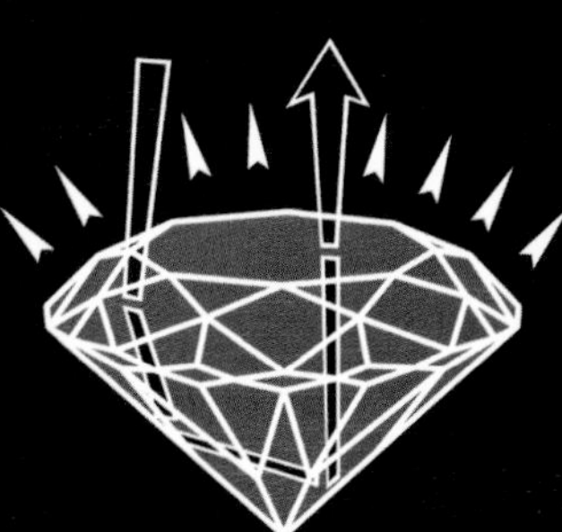

NAME: MATILDA

WHAT MAKES MATILDA MOVE: LIKE A LIGHT WAVE, SHE'S A GO-WITH-THE-FLOW KIND OF GAL—SHE BENDS AND MOVES TO ADAPT TO HER ENVIRONMENT

FAVORITE TACTIC: KEEP THE PEACE

PHYSICS AT PLAY: SNELL'S LAW DESCRIBES THE RELATIONSHIP BETWEEN THE ANGLES OF INCIDENCE AND REFRACTION WHEN A LIGHT WAVE PASSES THROUGH A BOUNDARY BETWEEN TWO DIFFERENT MEDIA, LIKE WATER AND GLASS.

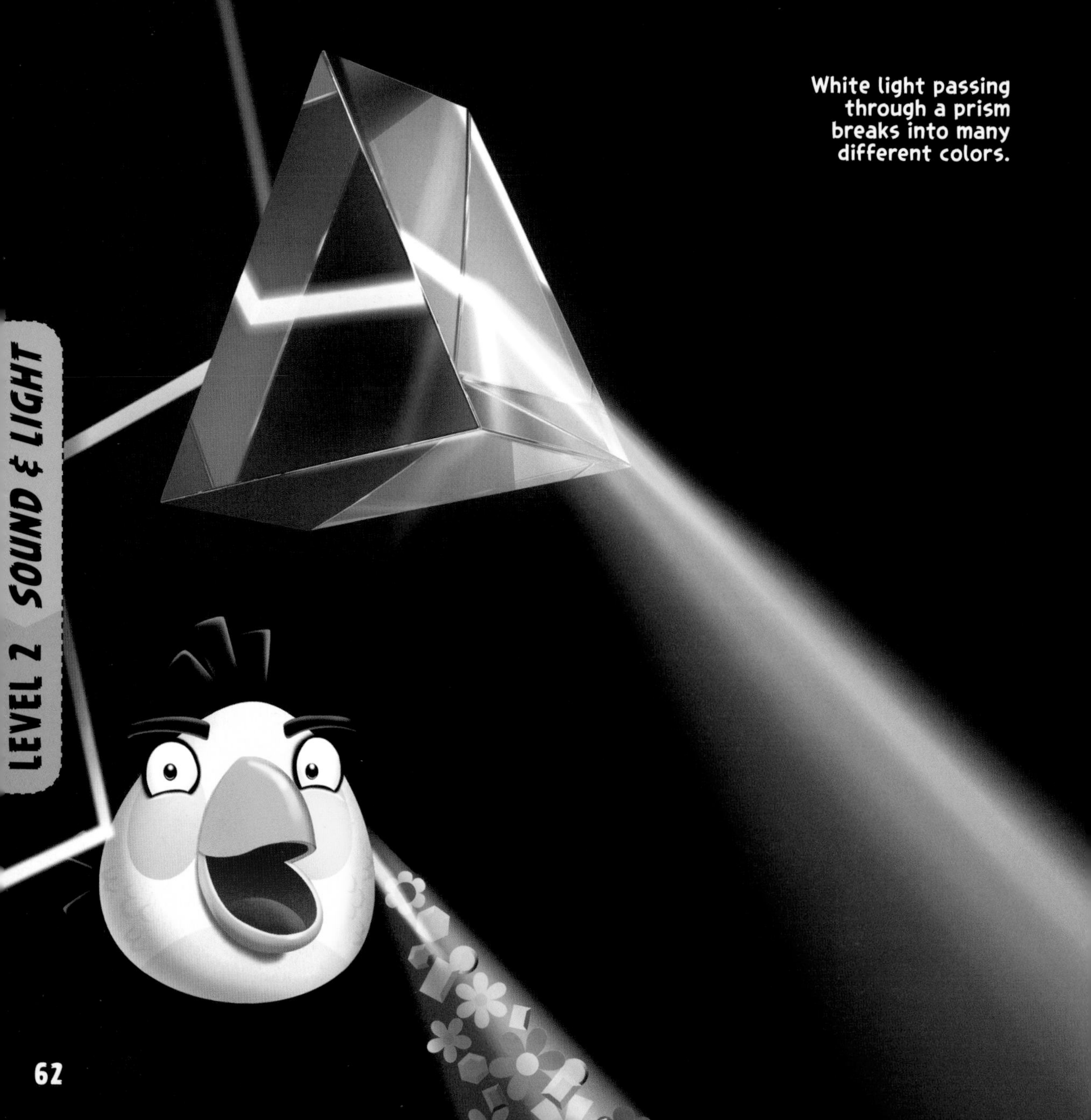

White light passing through a prism breaks into many different colors.

MIXING LIGHT

What happens when white light passes through glass? It bends. We call this *refraction.* And as it happens, different colors of light bend different amounts. If you have a piece of glass shaped correctly, you can get white light to separate into all the colors of the rainbow. Although they are continuously changing colors, we traditionally label them as red, orange, yellow, green, blue, and violet.

WHY DOES A RED APPLE APPEAR RED?

If you shine white light on an apple, the apple absorbs all the colors of the spectrum except red. Only the red reflects and enters your eye, so the apple appears red. But what would happen if you had a blue light shining on a red apple? Since there would be no red light to reflect, the apple wouldn't reflect *any* light. With no light reflecting off the apple, your eye would interpret it as being black.

PHYSI-FACTS

- VISIBLE LIGHT WAVELENGTHS ARE MEASURED IN UNITS OF NANOMETERS—THERE ARE A BILLION NANOMETERS IN ONE METER (3.3 FT).
- RED LIGHT HAS A WAVELENGTH OF AROUND 650 NANOMETERS.
- VIOLET LIGHT HAS A WAVELENGTH OF ABOUT 400 NANOMETERS.
- WHITE LIGHT CAN BE SPLIT INTO THE FUNDAMENTAL COLORS WITH EITHER A PRISM OR A DIFFRACTION GRATING.

RAINBOWS

Believe it or not, rainbows aren't made with magic unicorn dust. Instead, they are made with light and tiny drops of water. When light hits these droplets and goes from the air to inside the water drop, it refracts. Remember that when light refracts, different colors bend different

You often see rainbows after rain showers because they are formed when light hits water drops.

LEVEL 2 SOUND & LIGHT

amounts. Separated into all its component colors, the light reflects off the back of the water droplet and produces the rainbow effect.

ARE RAINBOWS JUST IN THE SKY?

You can make a rainbow at home. All you need is the sun and a water hose that can make some mist. Go out into a sunny part of your yard and have a friend spray the mist. Look at the mist from different angles until you can see the rainbow colors. Sadly, you won't find a pot of gold at the end.

PHYSI-FACTS

A SUN DOG IS SIMILAR TO A RAINBOW, BUT IT IS A VISIBLE SPOT TO THE SIDE OF THE SUN CAUSED BY ICE CRYSTALS IN THE SKY.

LIGHT BOTH REFLECTS AND REFRACTS WHEN IT HITS A SURFACE LIKE WATER.

AT CERTAIN ANGLES OF LIGHT, YOU CAN SEE A DOUBLE RAINBOW.

TELESCOPES CAN FOCUS LIGHT EITHER BY REFLECTING LIGHT WITH MIRRORS OR REFRACTING LIGHT WITH A LENS.

Leopards' eyes can appear as retro reflectors.

RETRO REFLECTORS

Have you ever looked at a wet road while driving on a dark night? It is difficult to see the road. Why is that? Remember from before that in order to see something, light has to enter the eye. When light interacts with nonshiny surfaces, it reflects light not just in one direction, but in all directions. But when light strikes shiny objects—like a wet road—the light reflects away at the same angle it hit the surface. This means that very little light enters your eye.

HOW CAN YOU MAKE THINGS EASIER TO SEE IN THE DARK?

If only there was some way to make light reflect back to where it came from. Maybe you can think of one way to do this—with a mirror. If you shine a flashlight right into a mirror, the light comes right back at you. However, if you shine at an angle, it does not come back.

How do you make it easier to see a road in the dark? The solution to this problem is the retro reflector. A retro reflector doesn't reflect light the same way a mirror does. Instead, it reflects light right back in the direction it came from. One way to make a retro reflector is to coat some material (like a stop sign) with tiny glass beads.

PHYSI-FACTS

- RETRO REFLECTORS ARE COMMONLY PLACED ON RUNNING SHOES.
- LARGER METAL RETRO REFLECTORS ARE USED TO MAKE SMALL BOATS MORE VISIBLE ON RADAR.
- ASTRONAUTS LEFT A RETRO REFLECTOR ON THE MOON. IT IS USED TO MEASURE THE EARTH-TO-MOON DISTANCE.
- YOU CAN BUY RETRO REFLECTOR TAPE TO ADD TO THINGS YOU WANT TO BE MORE VISIBLE AT NIGHT.

LEVEL 3 THERMODYNAMICS

The study of heat and its transformation to mechanical energy

Red gets to new heights!

PHYSICS AT PLAY

TAKE SOME SALT AND LOOK AT THE SMALLEST GRAIN. EVEN THIS TINY GRAIN IS A BILLION BILLION ATOMS (10^{18}).

WHAT IS MATTER?

If you take a rock and break it in half, you essentially get two smaller rocks. Could you keep doing this forever, breaking the rock into smaller and smaller rocks? It turns out that you cannot. Eventually you would get down to pieces that are, in a sense, unbreakable. These pieces are called *atoms.* If you like, you can think of these atoms as the fundamental building blocks for all objects. You wouldn't be able to actually *see* the atoms; they are *really* small. In fact, it would take over 1,000 trillion atoms to span the distance of the tip of a pin.

As I said, atoms are mostly unbreakable, but you *can* break them apart. If you did, you would find that they are all made of just three even smaller pieces: protons, electrons, and neutrons.

PHASES OF MATTER

Let's think of matter as being made up of tiny balls. Of course, this is just a model, but it's a useful model. For example, look at water.

Water—like most materials—can take on three phases of matter: liquid, gas, and solid. At room temperature, water is in the liquid phase. If it were possible to observe the water molecules, you would see them moving around each other while still staying close together. If you were to heat the water to boiling, it would turn to steam—a gas. In this gas phase, the molecules are moving around much more rapidly and can go farther from one another. Or, if you cooled the liquid water enough, it would freeze, becoming a solid. In the solid phase, the molecules are close together, very much like in the liquid phase.

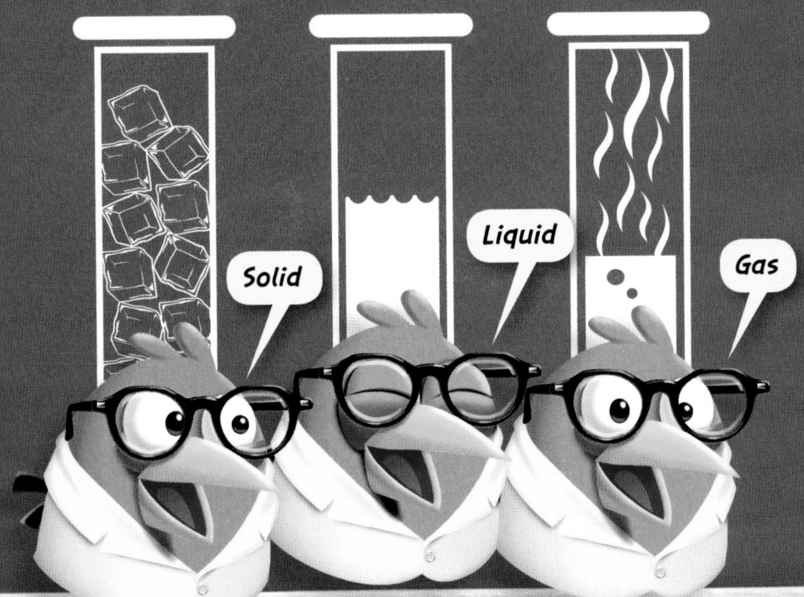

TEMPERATURE

Let's go back to the example of liquid water. What is the difference between cold and warm water? If you observed the water molecules, cool and warm water would look very similar—the big difference being that in the warmer water, the molecules would be moving around faster than in the cool water. In our tiny-ball model of matter, higher temperature materials have faster moving tiny balls.

Take a cold soda and set it on a warm table for some time. After a while, the table and soda will have the same temperature. They don't have the same energy; they just have the same temperature. Really, this is one way to define temperature. It is the property two objects share when in contact.

When two objects reach the same temperature, we call it *thermal equilibrium.* This is essentially how a thermometer works. You place it in something—like under your tongue—and after a while it reaches the same temperature as the object you wish to measure.

Heat can never pass from a colder to a warmer body without some other change, connected therewith, occurring at the same time. -RUDOLF CLAUSIUS

PRESSURE, VOLUME, & TEMPERATURE

I think we can all agree on a basic definition of *volume* as the space something takes up—except when we talk about a gas. The volume of gas usually depends on the volume of the container that holds the gas.

Pressure isn't quite as straightforward. It's easy to confuse pressure and force, but they are different. As an example, take your open hand and push on awall. Now push with the same force on the wall, but with just one finger. The force might be the same, but something is different. Since the contact area of the finger is smaller, it would have a greater pressure on the wall.

Gases also exert pressure on surfaces. In the tiny-ball model of gases, this pressure can be thought of as the balls bouncing off the walls of the container. If you increase the temperature of the gas, you get more and harder collisions with the walls, and therefore the pressure goes up.

I WONDER IF BOMB KNOWS ALL OF THIS . . .

Very high-temperature sparks from a fun sparkler

ENERGY VERSUS TEMPERATURE

Do higher temperature objects have more energy? It seems like that would be the case. In fact, if the molecules are moving faster, then they do have a higher *kinetic* energy. But while the particles in the material might have a higher kinetic energy, the *total* energy depends on how many particles are in the material.

WHY DO SOME HOT OBJECTS NOT BURN YOU?

Here's an example. You're probably familiar with sparklers used on the Fourth of July and for other celebrations. These sparklers shoot out glowing sparks that glow because they have a very high temperature—perhaps around 2000°F (1100°C). Then shouldn't these sparks burn you? Surprisingly, no. Even though the temperature of these flying sparks is high, they have a very low mass, which gives each spark a small amount of thermal energy and little ability to burn skin.

PHYSI-FACTS

WATER IS USEFUL AS A COOLANT BECAUSE IT TAKES A LARGE AMOUNT OF ENERGY TO CHANGE ITS TEMPERATURE.

IRON MELTS AT 2800°F (1540°C).

THE SURFACE OF THE APOLLO SPACE CAPSULE COULD REACH TEMPERATURES UP TO 5000°F (2760°C) DURING REENTRY.

IT TAKES ALMOST FOUR TIMES AS MUCH ENERGY TO CHANGE THE TEMPERATURE OF WATER AS IT DOES TO CHANGE THE TEMPERATURE OF THE SAME MASS OF STEEL.

TRANSFER OF THERMAL ENERGY

What would you consider to be a cold temperature? Certainly not a 70°F (21°C) breeze on a nice day, right? What about 70°F (21°C) water? Let me tell you, that is some cold water. Why does it feel so cold when really it is the same temperature as the air? Because our bodies don't actually "feel" temperature. Instead, we feel changes in thermal energy.

DOES ENERGY GO FROM HOT TO COLD OR COLD TO HOT?

How quickly is energy transferred? Well, this depends on the two materials and the difference in their temperatures. The greater the difference in temperature, the quicker the transfer of thermal energy occurs. The interesting thing is that when two objects are in contact, thermal energy always goes from the object with a higher temperature to the object with a lower temperature. You've seen this before when a cool soda sits on the counter. The soda will increase in thermal energy and this energy comes from the warmer surroundings.

PHYSI-FACTS

A CALORIE IS THE UNIT OF HEAT REQUIRED TO CHANGE THE TEMPERATURE OF ONE GRAM BY ONE DEGREE CELSIUS.

A 10-CALORIE PEANUT RELEASES 10,000 CALORIES OF ENERGY WHEN BURNED.

THE GULF STREAM CARRIES WARM WATER TO THE NORTH ATLANTIC OFF OF EUROPE, WHERE THE HEAT TRANSFERS TO THE AIR AND WARMS THE EUROPEAN CONTINENT.

Humans need extra insulation for protection in cold environments.

A traditional fire bow rubs wood together to start a fire.

FRICTION & THERMAL ENERGY

Any moving object has kinetic energy. But what happens when an object rubs against something such that it slows down? Remember that energy isn't destroyed, it just changes forms. So, if the kinetic energy decreases, but where does this energy go? When an object slows because of friction, there is an increase in thermal energy.

HOW CAN YOU START A FIRE WITH STICKS?

When you rub two sticks together, there is a friction interaction. You can use your muscles to keep the sticks moving at a constant speed, but there will be a continual transfer of energy to make both sticks warmer. If you keep it up for some time, they can get hot enough to start a fire.

PHYSICS AT PLAY

YOU DON'T NEED STICKS TO SEE THIS WORK. RUB YOUR HANDS TOGETHER VERY QUICKLY. NOW HOLD THEM UP TO YOUR CHEEKS. YOU SHOULD BE ABLE TO FEEL THAT YOUR HANDS HAVE GOTTEN WARMER.

FIRE

What is fire? Let's say you have a small piece of burning wood. Clearly it gives off energy both in the form of light and thermal energy. But where does this thermal energy come from? The ashes contain some of the same material that was in the wood. During the burning process, the wood has been broken down, and chemical energy is released in the form of heat.

WHAT DETERMINES THE COLOR OF A FLAME?

Why is there light energy? There are really two types of flames with different colors. For a candle or burning wood, the orange-tinted light comes from small particles of soot released from the wood. This soot gets very hot and glows just like any other hot object glows. If you look at the fire from a gas stove, it appears blue. There are no particles of soot, and therefore there is no orange-colored flame.

What about the shape of a flame? The fire heats up the air and this hotter air rises up to make the flame also reach upward. If you were able to light a match in a weightless environment, it would not be pointy but instead would expand spherically in all directions.

PHYSI-FACTS

FIRE NEEDS FUEL, HEAT, AND OXYGEN. REMOVE ANY ONE OF THESE AND YOU WILL KILL THE FIRE.

BURNING COAL RELEASES 24 MILLION JOULES FOR JUST A KILOGRAM OF FUEL.

A CANDLE WICK BRINGS MELTED WAX UP TO THE FLAME. THE FLAME BURNS THE WAX, NOT THE WICK.

Even Bomb's not that explosive!
Scientists release and burn methane trapped under the ice.

BOMB

BOMBS AWAY!

It's not easy being angry all the time, but what if one misstep could make you explode? Bomb does his best to keep his cool, but the sight of pigs is enough to ignite his fuse—and once Bomb gets fired up, there's no stopping him. He's as unstable as nitroglycerin, and the aftershock of his outbursts are equally devastating. Bomb may be the most efficient at eliminating enemies, but his fiery hot temper makes it hard to maintain friends. Best to keep your distance when this Angry Bird detonates.

ALFRED NOBEL

$C_3H_5N_3O_9$ (nitroglycerin)

NAME: BOMB

WHAT MAKES BOMB MOVE: INTERNAL PRESSURE

FAVORITE TACTIC: TOTAL ANNIHILATION

PHYSICS AT PLAY: ENERGY FROM THE COMPOUND'S DECOMPOSITION RELEASES ENERGY THAT CREATES A PRESSURE WAVE AND THIS DETONATES THE SURROUNDING FUEL.

PLASMA, THE FOURTH PHASE OF MATTER

Take some ice, some very cold ice. Now add energy to increase its temperature. Eventually, the ice will get to its melting point and change to liquid water. If you keep adding energy, the liquid water will again change its phase and become a gas.

WHAT HAPPENS WHEN YOU KEEP HEATING STEAM?

At a certain point, the energy of the water will be so great that the hydrogen and oxygen atoms will no longer stay together as a water molecule. Instead, you will just get a collection of independent hydrogen and oxygen atoms. Even at this point, it's possible to keep increasing the energy. Eventually the electrons in the atoms will become free and transform the material to a type of matter called *plasma.*

PHYSICS AT PLAY

ALTHOUGH IT MAY SEEM THAT YOU HARDLY EVER ENCOUNTER PLASMA MATERIALS, THE PLASMA STATE IS ACTUALLY THE MOST COMMON STATE OF MATTER IN THE UNIVERSE.

A plasma
globe lets you
interact with
plasma in a
safe manner.

MELTING ICE & MAKING ICE CREAM

LEVEL 3 THERMODYNAMICS

Ice can be very useful. It always has been. If you put ice in a glass of water, something happens. The ice actually melts and turns into liquid water. This change in phase requires additional energy. The only place this energy can come from is the water, so melting ice quickly decreases the temperature of the water.

CAN YOU MAKE ICE EVEN COLDER?

The one problem with ice is that you can't use it to get things colder than the freezing temperature of water—about 32°F (0°C). Actually, there is a cool trick (literally) that you can use to make both ice cream and safer roads. If you add salt to ice, it produces a chemical reaction that does two things. First, it makes the ice colder. This is useful for making homemade ice cream. Second, it lowers the temperature at which ice melts. This means that salt on an icy road can help the ice melt even if the temperature is below freezing.

PHYSI-FACTS

THE ENERGY NEEDED TO CHANGE SOLID ICE TO LIQUID WATER IS ABOUT TEN TIMES MORE THAN THE ENERGY NEEDED TO BRING THE SAME AMOUNT OF WATER TO A BOILING TEMPERATURE.

ADDING SALT TO ICE CAN GET THE TEMPERATURE DOWN TO 0°F (-18°C).

SALTED ICE CAN BE COLD ENOUGH TO "BURN" YOUR SKIN.

WATER IS ONE OF THE ONLY MATERIALS THAT FLOATS WHEN IT FREEZES.

Don't worry, there's more ice cream in the freezer.

Athletes prefer to wear clothes that allow sweat to pass through to assist in the cooling process.

It's always good to break a sweat!

COOLING BY EVAPORATION

You might not like to sweat, but it's very useful. When you sweat, your body releases water onto your skin. This water then takes heat energy from your body as it makes the phase transition from a liquid to a gas. When you lose thermal energy, you cool off. It might be a nuisance, but sweating really does cool you down.

DOES SWEATING ALWAYS WORK TO COOL YOU OFF?

Humidity makes a big difference in how well this process works. If it is humid, there is already a lot of water gas (we usually call it water vapor) in the air. In this case, not all of the sweat will evaporate. This leaves you with a sweaty shirt, and no one likes that. On the other hand, if the air is very dry, you might not even realize you are sweating, because the sweat evaporates completely and leaves your skin dry. In either case, you need to remember to drink plenty of fluids in hot weather to replace the water that your body loses by sweating.

PHYSICS AT PLAY

COOLING BY EVAPORATION ISN'T LIMITED TO PEOPLE. IF YOU TAKE A WET CLOTH AND PLACE IT OVER A BOTTLE OF WATER, THE WATER IN THE CLOTH WILL EVAPORATE AND COOL THE WATER INSIDE THE BOTTLE.

THERMAL EXPANSION

What would happen if you warmed up a cold balloon? In the tiny-ball model of the air inside the balloon, these balls would begin moving faster and faster as the temperature increases. Tiny balls moving faster means that they push more against the balloon and cause it to expand.

THERMAL EXPANSION CAN CAUSE PROBLEMS

In some cases, this thermal expansion can be an issue that needs to be addressed. On warm summer days, bridges get warmer and expand. Modern bridges include spaces to accommodate this expansion. Without the expansion joints, bridges would buckle in the summer heat.

In other cases, thermal expansion can be useful. Older style thermostats, for example, use a strip of metal to turn air-conditioning on and off. As the temperature rises, the strip of metal expands and acts as a switch to turn the AC on. As the temperature cools, the metal returns to its original size and turns off the AC.

PHYSICS AT PLAY

IN A WAY, YOU COULD SAY THAT THERMAL EXPANSION IS RESPONSIBLE FOR POPPING POPCORN. WHEN A CORN KERNEL IS HEATED RAPIDLY, THE WATER INSIDE TURNS TO STEAM. THIS STEAM CAUSES THE KERNEL TO "POP."

Water inside a kernel turns to steam and causes the pop in popcorn.

MIGHTY EAGLE

TOO HOT TO HANDLE

If Elvis was a hunk of burning love, Mighty Eagle is our hunk of burning anger, seething in his own frustration. Disillusioned by battles lost, this elder bird lives in solitude to hide his shame for failing to protect the eggs in days of yore. He conserves energy sitting undisturbed on his mountaintop, but if an inkling of anger starts percolating, beware the moment he boils over. Mighty Eagle's outbursts are seldom, but his rage is a heat wave that'll melt the mountains down.

NICOLAS LÉONARD SADI CARNOT

$$\Delta L = L_0 \alpha \Delta T$$

NAME: MIGHTY EAGLE

WHAT MAKES MIGHTY EAGLE MOVE: INTRUDERS—AND SARDINES—GET HIS MERCURY RISING.

FAVORITE TACTIC: COMBUSTION

PHYSICS AT PLAY: MATTER WILL CHANGE IN VOLUME IN RESPONSE TO A CHANGE IN TEMPERATURE.

INSULATORS

How do some mammals survive in extreme cold weather? If you put a warm animal next to cold snow, the animal should lose thermal energy rather quickly. Most mammals have fur because fur is a thermal insulator. Insulators decrease the rate that thermal energy is transferred from a hot object to a cold object. For animals with fur, the fur traps air near the skin. This trapped air then acts as an insulator, just like your winter coat.

Penguins have natural insulation from a combination of feathers and air. Humans, not so much.

DO BLANKETS JUST KEEP THINGS WARM?

What would happen if you took a wool blanket and put it over a cold soda? Would the drink warm up quicker than an uncovered soda? No—just the opposite. Remember, the wool blanket is an insulator. It slows down the transfer of thermal energy. In this case, it would slow the transfer of energy to the soda and keep it colder for a longer time. Basically, this is what an ice cooler does; if you like, you can put hot things in one and it will keep them warm also.

PHYSI-FACTS

TO STAY WARM IN WATER, PEOPLE WILL OFTEN WEAR A WETSUIT.

DOWN-FILLED COATS TRAP AIR TO HELP INSULATE FROM THE COLD.

A WETSUIT INSULATES YOU BY TRAPPING WATER BETWEEN YOUR SKIN AND THE WETSUIT MATERIAL, WHICH YOUR BODY WARMS TO BODY TEMPERATURE. THEN THE WETSUIT MATERIAL (USUALLY NEOPRENE) ACTS AS AN INSULATOR TO KEEP BOTH YOU AND YOUR WARM WATER WARM.

THE VERY COLDEST THINGS

Everyone knows that ice is cold. In Fahrenheit, it is 32 degrees or colder; in Celsius, zero or below. What—apart from the salted ice we discussed earlier—is colder than water ice? What about "dry ice"? Dry ice is very cold—it has to at least be 110 degrees *below* 0°F (-79°C) to be a solid.

HOW ABOUT SOME REALLY COLD THINGS?

You might think you would never need anything colder than dry ice, but that's not quite true. One particular application requires temperatures much colder than -100°F (-73°C): superconductors. A superconductor is a material that has interesting electrical and magnetic properties at very low temperatures. If you had to create an extremely strong magnetic field, just about the only way to do it would be by using superconductors. Why would you need these high magnetic fields? One common use is in medical imaging devices such as the MRI (Magnetic Resonance Imaging).

Most superconductors work at a temperature of -452°F (-269°C). If you thought dry ice was cold, this is unimaginably cold.

PHYSI-FACTS

THE SAME HELIUM YOU USE TO FILL BALLOONS IS USED TO RUN SUPERCONDUCTING MAGNETS IN MRIs.

WE GET MOST OF OUR HELIUM FROM DIFFERENT TYPES OF OIL DEPOSITS.

LIQUID NITROGEN ISN'T AS COLD AS LIQUID HELIUM. NITROGEN IS LIQUID AT A TEMPERATURE OF -321°F (-196°C).

A magnet can levitate over a superconducting material at very cold temperatures.

LEVEL 4 ELECTRICITY & MAGNETISM

A branch of physics dealing with charges and the attraction between objects

When camping close
to the Earth's poles,
you might see auroras
in the sky.

ELECTRIC & MAGNETIC FIELDS

It's really fun to play with magnets. Take two and bring them near each other. It almost feels like magic when the two magnets interact without even touching. The same can be done with electric charges. Rub a balloon on your shirt and bring it near your hair. The hair is attracted to the balloon, also without touching.

How can these things interact without contact? The answer is with fields. Around any magnet, there is a magnetic field. What is a field? If you like, you can think of a field as an area of influence that surrounds some object. When two magnets are close together, their magnetic fields can interact—no touching necessary. Electric charges do something similar when they make electric fields. What about gravity? You don't have to touch the Earth to be pulled by it. Yes, the Earth creates a gravitational field.

FUNDAMENTAL CHARGES

Pick up an apple or a pencil. These and every other object you can pick up are made of just three different particles. There is the negatively charged electron and the positively charged proton. The third object is the neutron, which has no electrical charge. Most objects have the same number of electrons and protons. This makes their total net charge zero or neutral.

The electron and proton are called the fundamental charges. Why? Let's think of an example. What if you take a balloon and rub it on your hair? Both your hair and the balloon will become electrostatically charged, because some of the electrons in your hair were transferred to the balloon. You can transfer one electron, or two electrons, or five billion electrons. However, you can't transfer one and a half electrons. The electron is the smallest amount of charge you can have, which is why we call it a fundamental charge.

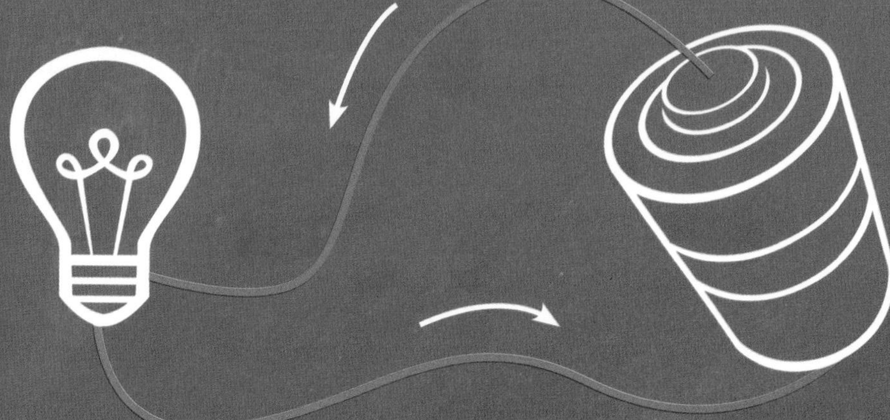

ELECTRIC CURRENT

Take a simple flashlight. When you turn it on, something happens to make the light bulb glow. In this case, there is an electric current flowing from the flashlight's battery, through the bulb, and back to the battery. But what is current? In almost all cases, electric current is the movement of negative charges. We often say "flow" when talking about current because many of the ideas of flowing water can be applied similarly to electric currents.

Think of water flowing through a pipe. If this water is used to turn a wheel, it is still the same water. The water does not get "used up." The same is true for electrical currents. The electrical current might do useful things, like light a light bulb or spin a motor, but the current doesn't get used up.

MAGNETS

If you play around with a bar magnet, you might notice a couple of things. First, the magnet has two different ends. We call these ends the "north" and "south" poles for reasons that I will explain later. If you bring the north end of a magnet near the north end of another magnet, they will repel each other.

What would happen if you cut a bar magnet into two pieces? It turns out that each piece would just be a smaller magnet with a north pole on one end and a south pole on the other. You can't have a single pole all by itself. If you have a north pole, there also has to be a south pole.

Grab a magnet and use it to examine its interactions with other materials. Are metals attracted? You will find that some metals are, in particular iron and steel. We call these materials *ferromagnetic*. Other materials like aluminum and copper do not interact with a magnet.

An electrostatically charged balloon interacts with a cat's fur.

STATIC ELECTRICITY

Does a charged balloon have extra negative charges or extra positive charges? Really, the only way you could determine this is by bringing it next to other objects with a known charge. Similarly charged objects repel and opposite charges attract.

WHAT HAPPENS WHEN A CHARGE IS NEAR A NEUTRAL OBJECT?

Suppose you rub a balloon on your shirt to give it a charge and then place the balloon close to the fur of a cat. The fur will be attracted to the balloon. The fur can be attracted to the charged balloon even if the fur is neutral. The charges can move around and make the positive charges get a little closer to the balloon than the negative charges. The closer charges have a stronger interaction, resulting in an attraction between the two objects. If you replaced the negative balloon with a positive piece of plastic, the exact same thing would happen.

PHYSICS AT PLAY

RUB A PLASTIC PEN OR COMB IN YOUR HAIR. NOW TEAR UP SOME PAPER INTO TINY PIECES AND PLACE THEM IN A PILE ON A TABLE. WHEN YOU BRING THE CHARGED PLASTIC NEAR THE PAPER, THEY WILL JUMP UP AND STICK TO THE PLASTIC.

GRAVITY VERSUS ELECTRICAL FORCES

Before, I said that the gravitational force was an interaction between objects that have mass (which is essentially everything you can think of). The electrical force is an interaction between objects that have electrical charge. There are two big differences.

IS GRAVITY OR ELECTRICAL FORCE STRONGER?

The more obvious difference between electrical charges and masses is that you can have repelling charges, but masses are always gravitationally attracted and never repel. This is because there are two types of charges (positive and negative) but only one kind of mass.

It turns out that the electric force interaction is significantly stronger than the gravitational interaction between particles. However, we tend to notice gravitational forces more often because of large objects like the Earth that have cumulative attractive forces.

PHYSI-FACTS

THE SUN EXERTS A GREATER GRAVITATIONAL FORCE ON THE MOON THAN DOES THE EARTH.

IN 1968, THE ASTRONAUTS IN APOLLO 8 WERE THE FIRST HUMANS TO LEAVE EARTH'S ORBIT.

BOTH GRAVITY AND ELECTRIC FORCES FOLLOW THE INVERSE-SQUARE LAW, DECREASING IN STRENGTH WITH DISTANCE.

IT IS POSSIBLE FOR A SMALL FOAM PEANUT TO ACCUMULATE ENOUGH STATIC CHARGE TO BALANCE THE GRAVITATIONAL FORCE AND FLOAT IN MIDAIR.

The moon orbits the Earth due to a gravitational interaction.

TERENCE

A BIRD WORTH 1,000 WORDS

If silence is golden, Terence is one highly valued bird. Haunted by bad memories, he refuses to speak and lives in seclusion. Terence channels his energy toward squashing anything in his path. Like metal to a magnet, Terence is attracted to his opponents, and he attacks with an electrifying charge. His current of fury creates an unstoppable force field, and his quiet approach takes his enemies by surprise until . . . *zap!*

MICHAEL FARADAY

$$E = -n \, d\Phi/dt$$

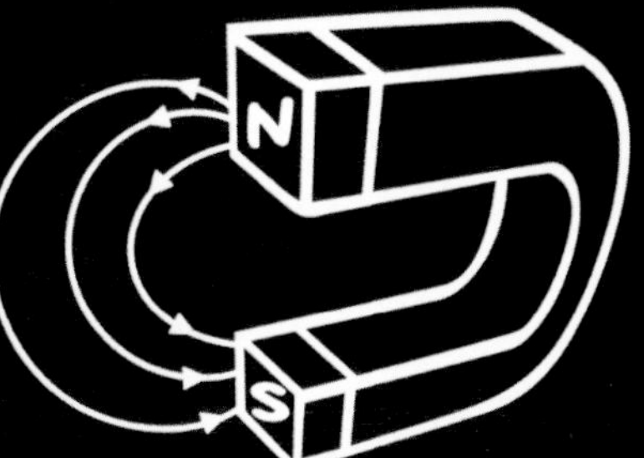

NAME: TERENCE

WHAT MAKES TERENCE MOVE: POSITIVES (HIS FELLOW BIRDS) AND NEGATIVES (PIGS)

FAVORITE TACTIC: NEVER SHOW WEAKNESS

PHYSICS AT PLAY: AN ELECTRICAL CURRENT IN A WIRE CREATES A CIRCULAR MAGNETIC FIELD AROUND THE WIRE, ITS DIRECTION (CLOCKWISE OR COUNTER-CLOCKWISE) DEPENDING ON THAT OF THE CURRENT.

ANIMALS & ELECTRICITY

Hey. I'm a shark, and this water sure is murky. If only there was some way to find fish to eat. Oh, but there is. Some animals—including sharks like the hammerhead—have the ability to detect electric fields.

WHY WOULD THERE BE ELECTRIC FIELDS AROUND FISH AND ANIMALS?

For many animals, the brain communicates to the muscles through a nervous system that uses electrical signals. It is these electrical signals, along with electrical charges on the animals' surface, that are detectable by some species of sharks and fish.

Other animals have the ability to generate an electrical voltage. The electric eel basically acts like many batteries connected together. With this, the eel can discharge the electricity to stun nearby prey.

ELECTRIC EELS CAN PRODUCE VOLTAGE EQUIVALENT TO 300 AAA BATTERIES.

BESIDES THE ELECTRIC EEL, THERE IS ALSO AN ELECTRIC RAY AND AN ELECTRIC CATFISH.

IN THE 1780S, LUIGI GALVANI FOUND THAT HE COULD MAKE DISSECTED FROGS' LEGS MOVE BY APPLYING ELECTRICITY.

A hammerhead shark has an odd-shaped head to help it detect prey.

A large junkyard electromagnet can be used to move pieces of steel.

ELECTRIC CURRENTS & MAGNETS

Do only magnets have magnetic fields? Actually, no. Electric currents also make magnetic fields. You have probably seen a simple electromagnet. It is just a coil of wire connected to a battery. If you wrap the wire around an iron nail, it will make an even better electromagnet. With it, you can pick up a few paper clips. When you disconnect the wire, the magnetic field turns off as well.

WHAT CAN YOU DO WITH ELECTRICITY AND MAGNETS?

Suppose you take another coil of wire and put it near a magnet. If the current in this wire keeps changing directions, it will alternatively push and then pull the magnet. With a high frequency of change in current, you also get high-frequency motion of the magnet. Can you guess what happens next? Sound! The vibrating magnet pushes the air to make sound. Just like that, you have a speaker.

PHYSI-FACTS

A JUNKYARD ELECTROMAGNET CAN BE STRONG ENOUGH TO LIFT A CAR.

THE ELECTROMAGNET WAS INVENTED IN 1824 BY WILLIAM STURGEON.

ELECTROMAGNETS ARE ALSO USED TO MAKE YOUR CELL PHONE VIBRATE.

MAGNET WIRE IS USED TO MAKE ELECTROMAGNETS. IT HAS A COATING TO MAKE THE ELECTRICAL CURRENT FORM LOOPS FOR A STRONGER MAGNETIC FIELD.

MAGNETS & ELECTRIC CURRENTS

It just doesn't seem fair that you can use electric current to make an electromagnet, but you can't use magnets to make an electric current. Wait! That's not true. Actually you *can* make an electric current with magnets. It turns out that a changing magnetic field will induce an electric current in a loop of wire.

WHAT CAN YOU DO WITH A MAGNET AND A WIRE?

Imagine there was some way to have a magnet continually turn around near a loop of wire. Of course, this would take some effort. You could have a person turn this magnet or maybe have the wind turn it on a windmill. In fact, this process is essentially what is used for almost all electricity generated by public utilities. Just about all power plants have some type of spinning magnet. They just use different methods to spin the magnet.

PHYSI-FACTS

MOST ELECTRICAL POWER PLANTS USE STEAM TO TURN A MAGNET, CREATING ELECTRICITY.

A COAL POWER PLANT BURNS COAL TO CREATE STEAM.

A NUCLEAR POWER PLANT USES A NUCLEAR REACTION TO CREATE STEAM.

IN 1821, MICHAEL FARADAY WAS ONE OF THE FIRST TO EXPLORE THE RELATIONSHIP BETWEEN MAGNETS AND ELECTRICITY.

Wind can be
used to turn
these giant
magnets with
coils of wires
to generate
electricity.
CAUTION
BIRDS:
WATCH FOR
SPINNING
BLADES!

A magnetic compass is what people used to navigate before smartphones.

THE EARTH AS A MAGNET

Ancient travelers could use a lodestone to help them with direction. The lodestone was a certain type of rock. If you suspended it from a string, it would end up always pointing the same direction, north, no matter where you stood. You may have already guessed that the lodestone was a type of naturally occurring magnetic rock. This was one of the first forms of a magnetic compass.

WHY DOES A COMPASS NEEDLE POINT NORTH?

If you have two magnets near each other, the north end of one will be attracted to the south end of the other. Opposites attract. The same thing happens with a magnetic compass. The rotating needle in the compass is just a tiny magnet. The north end of this needle is attracted to the south end of another giant magnet that we like to call "Earth."

PHYSICS AT PLAY

TO MAKE YOUR OWN COMPASS TAKE A STEEL NAIL OR NEEDLE AND DRAG ONE END OF A MAGNET ACROSS IT. NOW PLACE THE NAIL OR NEEDLE ON SOMETHING THAT CAN FLOAT IN WATER. THE NEEDLE SHOULD TURN TO POINT NORTH.

AURORAS & THE SOLAR WIND

There is another cool phenomenon that shows the magnetic properties of the Earth: the northern and southern lights, otherwise known as the aurora borealis and aurora australis, respectively. These lights show an amazing interaction between the sun and the Earth.

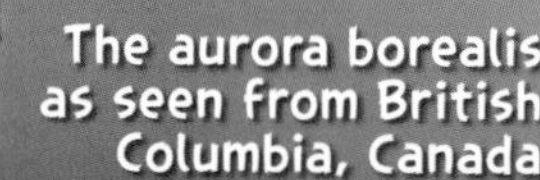
The aurora borealis as seen from British Columbia, Canada

The sun produces more than just light. On a regular basis, the sun ejects electrically charged particles—mostly protons and electrons—that we call the *solar wind*. Charged particles in motion are essentially the same thing as an electric current. And remember what happens when you have a current in a magnetic field? Yes, there is an interaction.

HOW DOES THE SOLAR WIND PRODUCE LIGHT?

The Earth's magnetic field near the poles is strong enough to cause the charged particles from the solar wind to interact with the air. These charged protons collide with the atoms in the air in such a way that light is produced. This is very similar to the way that a fluorescent bulb produces light. The color of light produced by the bulb depends on the type of gas inside (usually mercury vapor) and the type of coating on the glass. How actually does this process produce light? We will talk about this and the atom a little bit later.

THE EARTH'S MAGNETIC FIELD PREVENTS MUCH OF THE SOLAR WIND FROM REACHING THE SURFACE OF THE EARTH.

THE SOLAR WIND IS CONSIDERED A FORM OF RADIATION AND CAN BE HARMFUL TO HUMANS.

A TYPICAL REFRIGERATOR MAGNET IS ABOUT 100 TIMES STRONGER THAN THE EARTH'S MAGNETIC FIELD.

ALTHOUGH WE THINK OF THE EARTH'S MAGNETIC FIELD AS BEING PARALLEL TO THE GROUND, IT ALSO HAS A DOWNWARD COMPONENT, ESPECIALLY AT THE POLES.

THE BLUES

ALL FOR ONE AND ONE FOR ALL

Fresh from the nest, this trio is always in search of adventure, and they never shy away from an opportunity to make some sparks fly. Something truly spectacular happens when the Blues' powers combine. The Earth's auroras are one example of energies colliding, but when the Blues unite, it's enough to brighten even the Angry Birds' skies for days. Speed, intensity, and teamwork are all part of their dazzling display.

KRISTIAN BIRKELAND

1.5×10^6K = Approximate temperature of the solar wind

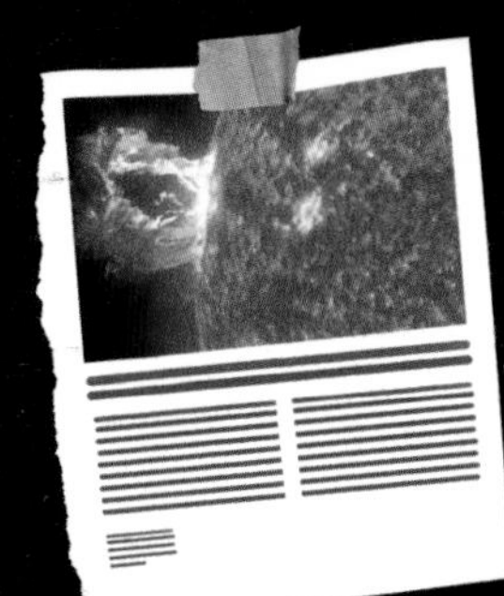

NAME: THE BLUES

WHAT MAKES THE BLUES MOVE: EACH OTHER

FAVORITE TACTIC: UNITE AND CONQUER

PHYSICS AT PLAY: SLOW SOLAR WIND, BELIEVED TO ORIGINATE FROM AROUND THE SUN'S EQUATORIAL BELT, CAN ESCAPE THE SUN'S GRAVITY BECAUSE OF ITS HIGH KINETIC ENERGY AND THE HIGH TEMPERATURES OF THE CORONA.

The Shanghai Maglev Train is the fastest passenger train currently in service.
These trains have nothing on me!
Shanghai Transrapid

MAGLEV TRAINS

Trains are pretty fascinating, but it isn't the easiest thing in the world to get them going really fast. There is always a large friction force being introduced by the wheels. One way to reduce this friction would be to take away the wheels. No contact between the wheels and the track would mean no friction.

HOW DO YOU MAKE A TRAIN WITHOUT WHEELS?

We know that two magnets with the same pole facing each other (like north to north) will repel. This is essentially how a maglev train goes over a track, hovering without actually touching it. However, how exactly do you make the train speed up?

To control its speed, a maglev train uses electromagnets both to suspend it above the track as well as to accelerate the train. By placing a series of conducting coils along the track, current can be run through them to make electromagnets in front of the train attract magnets on the train itself. Electromagnets behind the train repel and push it forward. The energy usage for this type of train can be considerably smaller than for a conventional one.

PHYSICS AT PLAY

BUILD YOUR OWN MAGLEV TRAIN. ONE WAY TO DO THIS IS WITH MAGNETIC TAPE. LAY THE TAPE DOWN IN SOME TYPE OF TRACK WITH SIDE WALLS SUCH AS A PLASTIC RAIN GUTTER AND PLACE A SMALL CERAMIC MAGNET OVER THE TRACK.

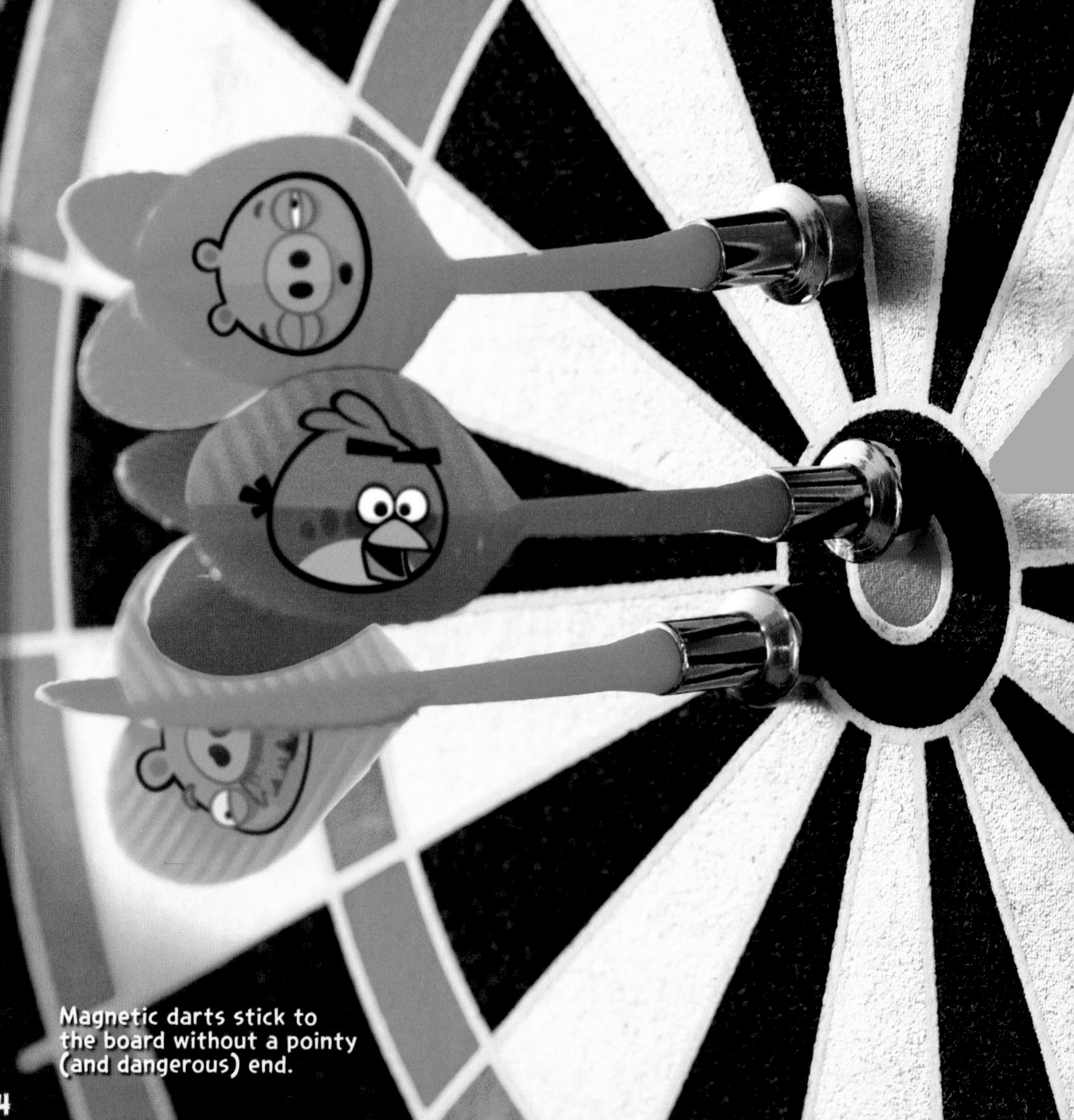

Magnetic darts stick to the board without a pointy (and dangerous) end.

MAGNETIC MATERIALS

Why do some iron objects act like magnets while others don't? It has to do with what we call *magnetic domains.* Imagine that a piece of iron is made of many tiny magnets—which essentially it is. If all of these tiny magnets are lined up the same way (with the north poles of the tiny magnets in the same direction), the iron will act like a magnet.

WHAT ARE THE TINY MAGNETS?

The tiny magnets are actually the atoms in the iron material. The electrons in these atoms act like tiny loops of electrical current that create magnetic fields. Other materials (like copper) have electrons that also create electric fields, but they have configurations in which the magnetic fields mostly cancel.

PHYSICS AT PLAY

YOU CAN MAKE MAGNETIC DOMAINS LINE UP IN AN IRON OR STEEL NAIL. TAKE ONE END OF A PERMANENT MAGNET AND DRAG THE MAGNET FROM THE HEAD TO THE TIP OF THE NAIL. NOW THE NAIL WILL ACT LIKE A WEAK MAGNET.

METAL DETECTORS

You are probably familiar with metal detectors or have seen someone using one to look for metal objects near the surface of the ground. How does this detector work? A basic metal detector uses two coils of conducting wire. One coil has an oscillating electrical current. This

A metal detector can be used to find lost treasures buried in the sand.

oscillating electrical current creates an oscillating magnetic field. Now, what happens when you have a changing magnetic field in the vicinity of an object that conducts electricity? It will create a current, which in turn will create its own magnetic field.

HOW DOES A METAL DETECTOR FIND METAL OBJECTS?

That's where the second coil comes in. The second coil of wire in the detector is used to detect the induced magnetic field from a piece of metal under the ground. This will work for any hidden object that is a conductor of electric current. That means that the detector can find all types of metals—not just magnetic metals like iron—so maybe you'll find some buried treasure and strike it rich!

PHYSI-FACT

METAL DETECTORS ARE OFTEN USED TO HUNT FOR METEORITES. MOST EARTH-BASED ROCKS DO NOT CONTAIN METAL, BUT MANY METEORITES HAVE A HIGH IRON CONTENT. SINCE IRON CONDUCTS ELECTRICITY, IT CAN BE FOUND WITH A METAL DETECTOR.

LEVEL 5 PARTICLE PHYSICS & BEYOND

A branch of science observing the existence of particles such as matter or radiation

The Andromeda
Galaxy, approximately
2.5 million light-years
from Earth

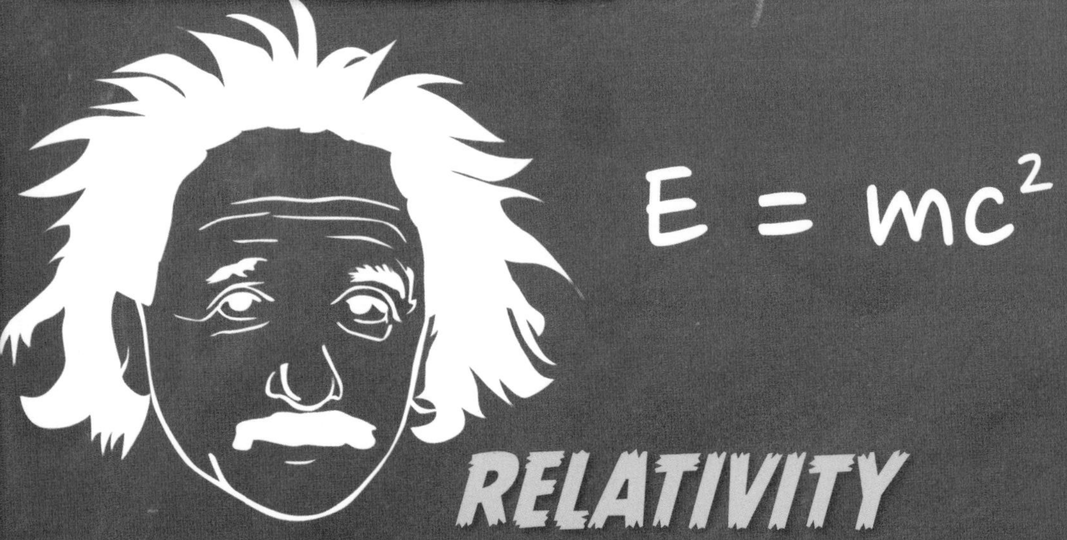

RELATIVITY

When objects move at very high speeds, we have to think about things in a slightly different way. To a stationary observer, the superfast object would appear different than it does to an observer moving alongside the fast object. Time would appear to change at a slower rate in the fast object. It would also appear to have different length measurements and even mass.

We say that events are relative. Time, energy, and mass are all relative to the speed of the observer. It seems crazy, but what that really means is that there is no preferred reference frame in the universe.

But how fast is superfast? Objects have a maximum speed limit: the speed of light (300 million meters per second or 186,000 miles per second). Things with mass just can't go faster than (or even as fast as) light. These ideas about relativity are true no matter what speed objects are moving at. However, unless their speed is at least 10 percent the speed of light, you would never notice it.

OBSERVING THE SUPERSMALL

Take a magnifying glass and look at a piece of hair. It looks pretty cool, and you can see some details that you couldn't see with just your eye. But what if you want to look at even smaller things? What if you want to look at the cells that make up the hair? You could do this with a microscope. Can you look at even smaller things? Can you look at the molecules that make up the cell? Well, you can "look" at them, but you won't be able to see them.

It turns out that using the visible spectrum of light can only work so far. Very small objects, like molecules, can't be imaged with visible light. The light in the colors we see just doesn't reflect off individual molecules. To observe things this small and smaller, we have to use some tricks. An electron microscope uses a beam of electrons instead of visible light to create images of very small objects.

BASIC BUILDING BLOCKS OF NATURE

You've probably built a castle or a car or a rocket out of toy blocks. What is it made of? Well, you can see that it is made of little building blocks. But what are the *blocks* made of? The answer depends on the material. If they are aluminum blocks, then the blocks are made of aluminum atoms. Plastic blocks would be made from a combination of different molecules. These molecules would in turn be made of atoms—mostly carbon atoms. And as we mentioned earlier, if we break down atoms, they are all made of electrons, protons, and neutrons. So, you could say that all ordinary matter is made of just these three things.

But why stop there? Can you break down an electron into other things? Well, we don't know. At this point, we say that the electron is a fundamental particle and is not made of smaller things. Protons and neutrons, on the other hand, *can* be described in terms of smaller pieces. We call these smaller pieces *quarks.*

WE USE STRONG FORCE TO TAKE DOWN THE PIGS!

FUNDAMENTAL INTERACTIONS

We have already looked at some fundamental interactions—in particular, the electromagnetic force and the gravitational force. There are two other fundamental forces. One is the weak nuclear force. This interaction is responsible for phenomena such as neutron decay. If you have an isolated neutron, it will eventually undergo a reaction and turn into a proton, an electron, and another fundamental particle—the *neutrino.*

The last fundamental force is the strong nuclear force. Consider the nucleus of the helium atom. It has two protons and two neutrons in it. The two protons are very close to each other and have the same positive electric charge, resulting in a very large electric force pushing them apart. Then, why do they stay together? There must be another force holding them together—and it has to be very strong. This is why the last fundamental force is called the strong nuclear force. It is an interaction between a group of particles we call *hadrons.* Both the proton and the neutron are hadrons.

An illustration of our galaxy, the Milky Way Galaxy

YOU ARE HERE.

SCALE OF THE UNIVERSE

What is the size of a salt crystal? Small. What is the size of an atom? It is also small. Hmm. Our language lacks words to describe just *how* small some of these things are.

The same thing happens when we talk about the very large. The Earth is large. The solar system is vastly larger. But what about a galaxy?

HOW DO WE DESCRIBE THE VERY SMALL AND VERY LARGE?

Instead of describing the size of an atom in units of inches or meters, we can use the nanometer unit. There are 1 billion nanometers in 1 meter (3.3 ft). With this unit, we can say that an atom is about 0.1 nanometers across.

When talking about the very large, we can use units of light-years. One light-year is the distance light travels in one year. Since light travels at about 300 million meters per second, this would be the same as 9 quadrillion (million billion) meters.

PHYSICS AT PLAY

ONE OTHER WAY TO DESCRIBE THE VERY EXTREME IS WITH SCIENTIFIC NOTATION. WE REPRESENT A NUMBER IN TERMS OF A BASE 10 AND THE NUMBER OF ZEROS THAT FOLLOW IT. ONE MILLION (1,000,000) WOULD BE WRITTEN AS 1×10^6.

ORIGIN OF THE UNIVERSE

Remember the Doppler effect? We talked about it in regard to sound waves, but it also works with light. If an object is moving away from us at a very high speed, the light from this object appears shifted toward longer wavelengths. We call this a *redshift*. Objects moving toward us have a light toward shorter wavelengths, a *blueshift.*

HOW DO MOST GALAXIES MOVE?

In 1929, Edwin Hubble noticed something about galaxies and redshifts. First, almost all of the galaxies were moving away from us. Second, the farther away the galaxy was, the greater its redshift. This information suggested that the universe was expanding. And if the universe is expanding, then it had to start from somewhere—the big bang.

PHYSICS AT PLAY

YOU CAN SIMULATE AN EXPANDING UNIVERSE WITH A BALLOON THAT IS PARTIALLY INFLATED. DRAW SOME DOTS ON ITS SURFACE WITH A MARKER. NOW ADD MORE AIR TO THE BALLOON SO THAT IT EXPANDS. THE DISTANCE BETWEEN ALL OF THE DOTS EXPANDS, JUST LIKE THE UNIVERSE. EVERYTHING GETS FARTHER APART.

Cosmic microwave background radiation is thermal radiation produced shortly after the big bang that fills the entire observable universe.

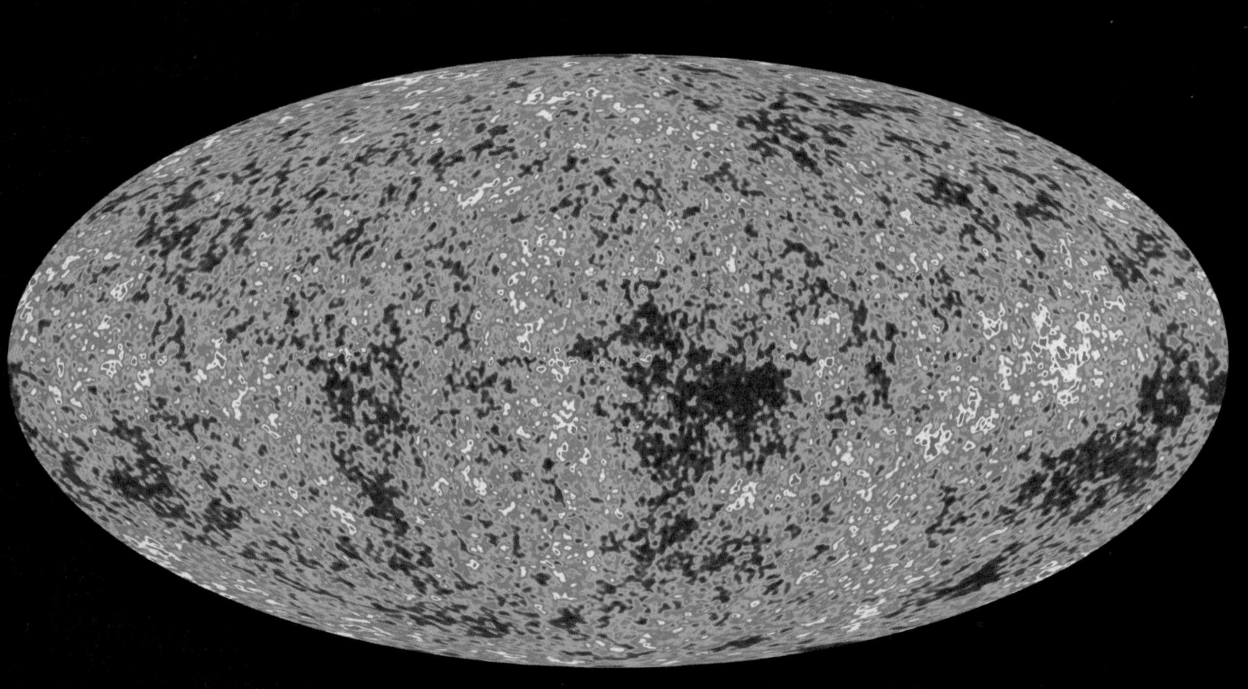

A giant cloud of space gas called the Carina Nebula

MATERIALS IN THE UNIVERSE

What if you were able to take a survey of all the elements in the universe? You would find that the most common element is hydrogen, followed by helium. They are the simplest elements.

HOW DO YOU MAKE ALL THE ELEMENTS?

All nuclei are made of protons and neutrons, but it is necessary that they have enough energy until they can get close enough for the strong nuclear force to keep them together. Of course, the process isn't that simple, but you get the idea. This same process of combining elements can be continued, but it will only get you so far. After you get 26 protons in an atom (this would be iron) it takes energy to make heavier elements like gold and plutonium. Where does this energy come from? It comes from highly energetic cosmic events such as the explosion of a star.

PHYSI-FACTS

AFTER HYDROGEN AND HELIUM, THE NEXT TWO MOST ABUNDANT ELEMENTS IN THE UNIVERSE ARE CARBON AND OXYGEN.

THE MOST ABUNDANT ELEMENT IN THE EARTH'S CRUST IS OXYGEN.

THE MOST ABUNDANT ELEMENT IN THE ATMOSPHERE IS NITROGEN.

ALL THE KNOWN ELEMENTS ARE DISPLAYED IN THE PERIODIC TABLE OF THE ELEMENTS.

THE LARGE HADRON COLLIDER

I'm kind of a collider, too!

How do you explore the structure of a proton? Protons are much too small to examine with any type of microscope, so scientists have to use other means. The Large Hadron Collider (LHC), operated by the European Organization for Nuclear Research (CERN), looks at matter by smashing them at speeds near the speed of light.

HOW DO YOU GET THESE PARTICLES UP TO SUCH HIGH SPEEDS?

The basic idea is to use the electric charge of the particles to give them an accelerating boost. This can get the hadrons only so fast before running out of space, though. The solution to this problem is to run the hadrons through the accelerator portion of the LHC multiple times in a circular path. The LHC uses large superconducting magnets to curve the particles around in a 17-mile (27 km) circle. This makes it one of the largest science projects on Earth.

PHYSI-FACTS

THE LHC USES MORE THAN 1,500 SUPERCONDUCTING MAGNETS.

THE LHC'S MAGNETS NEED TO BE AT A TEMPERATURE OF -456°F (-271°C).

THE LHC'S MAIN BEAM IS 300 FEET UNDERGROUND AND RUNS UNDER THE BORDER OF FRANCE AND SWITZERLAND.

CERN WAS THE FIRST INSTITUTION TO FIND EVIDENCE FOR THE HIGGS BOSON, IN 2012.

This large device is a particle detector at CERN.

An illustration of the interactions with matter near a black hole

BLACK HOLES

A typical star is an example of a balancing act. Gravity continually tries to squeeze it down into nothing. But the core is very hot due to nuclear fusion, and this hot material exerts outward pressure, preventing the star from collapsing. But what happens when the star stops its fusion process? The interior pressure is no longer enough to balance the gravitational force, and the star collapses. In some cases, it becomes a black hole.

WHY IS IT BLACK? IS IT REALLY A HOLE?

Without anything to stop it, the gravitational force can take a typical star and squeeze it down to the size of a small town—about 2 miles (3.2 km) across. At this size, the gravitational field is very strong—so strong that nothing can escape it, not even light. What happens when there is no light leaving something? It looks black. Is it a hole? Not really. It's just a superdense object.

PHYSI-FACTS

- A BLACK HOLE WITH THE SAME MASS AS THE SUN WOULD BE JUST 4 MILES (6.5 KM) ACROSS.
- THE GRAVITATIONAL FIELD AROUND A BLACK HOLE IS SO STRONG THAT IT CAN CAUSE LIGHT TO BEND.
- IT IS LIKELY THAT AN EXTREMELY MASSIVE BLACK HOLE IS AT THE CENTER OF OUR GALAXY.
- ACCORDING TO SCIENTIST STEPHEN HAWKING, BLACK HOLES SLOWLY EVAPORATE.

This lighted sign shows how different gases in the tubes make different colors.

ENERGY LEVELS & LIGHT

Neon signs have a distinctive orange color. The light works by sending high-speed electrons into neon gas in the tube. When the electron interacts with the neon atoms, it excites the neon to a higher energy level. The neon atom then decreases in energy again and gives off light in the process.

WHAT IF YOU EXCITED A DIFFERENT GAS?

If you replace the neon gas with hydrogen gas, a similar thing happens. However, there is something different: the color. In an atom, there is the positive nucleus surrounded by electrons. It turns out that these electrons exist in a number of discrete energy levels. When an electron jumps down an energy level, this corresponds to a particular color of light. Different atoms have unique energy levels, producing different colors.

PHYSICS AT PLAY

BY LOOKING AT THE COLOR OF LIGHT DIFFERENT OBJECTS PRODUCE, WE CAN DETERMINE WHAT ELEMENTS THESE OBJECTS CONTAIN. THIS WAY WE CAN EXPLORE DISTANT STARS WITHOUT EVEN GOING TO THEM.

NUCLEAR REACTIONS

In 1905, Albert Einstein suggested that there is a correlation between mass and energy. This led to his famous equation, $E = mc^2$. Here, E is energy, m is the mass of some material, and c is the speed of light.

HOW DO YOU CONVERT MASS TO ENERGY?

You can't just take a baseball or some other object and turn it into energy. Really, it's a good thing you can't. That would be more energy than anyone could handle. However, you can take an atom like uranium and use it to make energy. If a uranium atom is hit with a neutron, the atom can break apart into two lower-mass atoms. But here is the strange part: If you add up the mass of the resulting pieces, they have less mass than the original uranium atom. Where did the rest of the mass go? It was converted into energy. This is the process of that occurs in a nuclear reactor. The excess energy is used to make steam that turns a turbine in an electric generator.

PHYSI-FACTS

IF ALL MASS COULD BE CONVERTED TO ENERGY IN A NUCLEAR REACTOR, IT COULD PROVIDE 3 MEGAWATTS OF ELECTRICITY FOR A WHOLE YEAR WITH JUST 1 GRAM (0.035 OUNCE) OF MASS.

WHEN A NUCLEUS BREAKS INTO SMALLER PIECES, WE CALL THIS *NUCLEAR FISSION*.

FOR A LOWER-MASS NUCLEUS, YOU CAN GET ENERGY BY COMBINING ATOMS. THIS IS CALLED *NUCLEAR FUSION*.

THE WORLD'S FIRST NUCLEAR POWER PLANT WAS IN IDAHO AND BEGAN RUNNING IN 1951.

The cooling tower portion of a nuclear power plant in Washington State

These bubble paths are made by charged particles curving in a magnetic field.

ANTIMATTER

An electron is a small negatively charged particle. There is another particle that is very similar to the electron except that it has a positive charge. We call this the *positron,* and it is the antimatter version of the electron. There are antimatter versions of the other particles, too. For instance, there is the *antiproton.*

WHAT HAPPENS WHEN ANTIMATTER MEETS MATTER?

When you have a positron near an electron, their opposite charges cause them to be attracted. What is to prevent them from crashing into each other? Nothing. When these two particles meet, we say they *annihilate:* The two particles are converted into massive amounts of energy.

There is a mystery, though. At the beginning of the universe—the big bang—both matter and antimatter were created. But when we look around now, almost everything is made of matter and not antimatter. So what happened? Much of the original antimatter combined with normal matter, but there is some type of preference for normal matter. This is one of the questions the LHC is trying to answer.

IN 2010, THE U.S. USED MORE THAN 27,000 TERAWATT-HOURS OF ELECTRICAL ENERGY (OVER 10^{16} JOULES).

IF THIS ENERGY ALL CAME FROM ANTIMATTER ANNIHILATION, IT WOULD TAKE JUST ABOUT 100 GRAMS (0.22 LB) OF ANTIMATTER.

BANANAS CONTAIN THE RADIOACTIVE ELEMENT POTASSIUM. THE DECAY OF POTASSIUM CAN OCCASIONALLY PRODUCE A POSITRON.

IN 2010, CERN WAS ABLE TO COMBINE AN ANTIPROTON AND POSITRON TO MAKE AN ANTI-HYDROGEN ATOM.

DARK MYSTERIES

There are many people who think humans have pretty much figured out all the important questions. Not so. In fact, there are many things for which we don't even know what questions to ask. One mystery comes from the observation of galaxies. Astronomers see that there is more mass in the universe than we can account for. We call the mass that's missing "dark matter."

WHAT IS DARK MATTER?

No one knows for sure what other matter is in galaxies to account for their higher mass. One idea is that there are particle pairs to the existing Standard Model particles. What is the Standard Model? This is our basic description of matter and interactions. It includes particles such as the quarks and leptons, along with the fundamental interactions.

PHYSI-FACTS

- THE STANDARD MODEL INCLUDES 12 FUNDAMENTAL PARTICLES ALONG WITH THE 4 FUNDAMENTAL INTERACTIONS.
- SOME OF THEM HAVE AWESOME NAMES LIKE THE MUON AND THE CHARM QUARK.
- DARK ENERGY IS A THEORETICAL TYPE OF ENERGY THAT CAUSES THE UNIVERSE TO EXPAND.
- DARK MATTER MAKES UP ABOUT 23 PERCENT OF THE UNIVERSE.

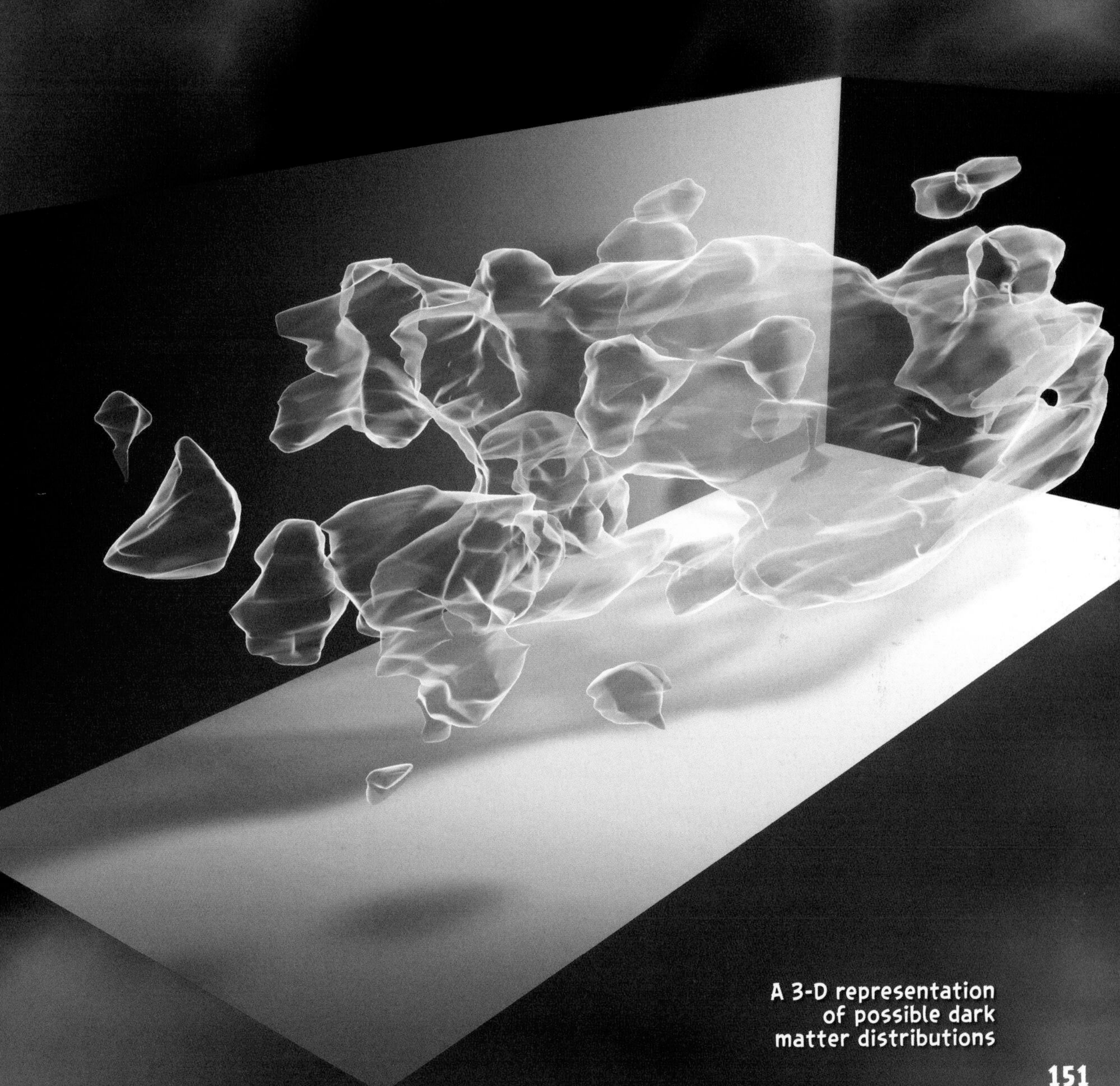

A 3-D representation of possible dark matter distributions

A view inside the Super-K neutrino detector showing scientists working on light detectors

NEUTRINOS

I prefer neutriyeses!

Neutrinos have very low mass compared to other particles—even electrons. Further, neutrinos have a neutral electric charge. This makes them very difficult to detect. In order to detect them, you need a lot of matter to see an occasional interaction. One way scientists do this is with vast amounts of water. This water is shielded from other forms of radiation by putting it deep underground. Then, with many, many light detectors, they look for small flashes of light emitted when a neutrino has an interaction.

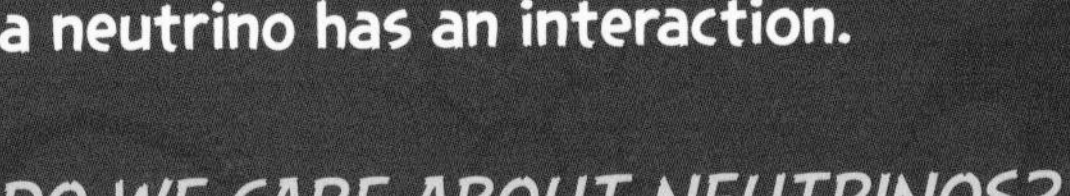

WHY DO WE CARE ABOUT NEUTRINOS?

How do you observe the interactions in the interior of the sun? You can't see in there, and you probably wouldn't want to go into the core of the sun. Instead, you have to look at the only thing that gets out of the interior of the sun—neutrinos. By studying the types and amounts of solar neutrinos, we can get a better idea of what happens inside the sun.

- THE SUN PRODUCES MANY NEUTRINOS IN THE FUSION PROCESS IN THE CORE.
- ABOUT 400 BILLION NEUTRINOS PER SECOND PASS THROUGH EACH SQUARE CENTIMETER (0.16 SQ IN) ON EARTH.
- SUPER-KAMIOKANDE (SUPER-K) IS A NEUTRINO DETECTOR 1,000 METERS (0.62 MI) UNDERGROUND IN JAPAN.
- SUPER-K USES 50,000 TONS OF WATER ALONG WITH 11,000 LIGHT SENSORS.

TRAVELING NEAR THE

The Large Hadron Collider accelerates particles up to very high speeds. A proton can have a speed of 99.999991 percent of the speed of light. But why not faster than this? Let's start with a different example. Suppose you have a tennis ball shooter that can fire a ball. If you double the speed, it has four times the energy.

WHAT HAPPENS WHEN YOU INCREASE THE SPEED OF A PROTON?

The idea that kinetic energy is proportional to the square of the speed is very useful—but it isn't exactly correct. If you keep going faster and faster, you will find that it no longer takes four times as much energy to double the speed. It will actually take more. The closer a particle's speed gets to the speed of light, the greater the amount of energy is needed to accelerate it. This is why the LHC doesn't have particles going at the speed of light or faster. It would take an infinite amount of energy.

A visualization of the path of cosmic rays as they enter Earth's atmosphere

SPEED OF LIGHT

PHYSI-FACTS

IT TAKES LIGHT EIGHT MINUTES TO GET FROM THE SUN TO THE EARTH.

GALILEO GALILEI IN 1638 WAS ONE OF THE FIRST TO ATTEMPT TO MEASURE THE SPEED OF LIGHT.

AT THEIR HIGHEST SPEED, PROTONS IN THE LHC CAN GO AROUND THE 17-MILE (27 KM) ACCELERATOR MORE THAN 11,000 TIMES IN JUST ONE SECOND.

GLOSSARY

Acceleration the rate that velocity changes

Annihilation the reaction in which a particle and its antiparticle collide and disappear (as with an electron and positron), releasing energy

Antimatter fundamental particles with the same mass as their normal matter equivalents, but the opposite electric charge

Antiproton the antimatter partner for the proton, with the same mass but a negative charge

Atom a unit of matter and the smallest unit of an element that still has the properties of that element

Black hole a very dense object with a gravitational field strong enough to prevent light from escaping

Blueshift the apparent shift in color toward shorter wavelengths of an object moving toward an observer at a very high speed

CERN the European Organization for Nuclear Research, operator of the Large Hadron Collider

Circular motion motion in which the object changes its direction at a continuous rate

Dark matter unknown material in the universe that has a gravitational influence on the motion of galaxies

Doppler effect the phenomenon of sound pitch shifting due to the motion of the sound's source

Echolocation the process of listening for reflected sound pulses to determine the distance of objects, as used by dolphins and other animals

Energy a measured quantity that is conserved in a closed system, such as kinetic energy, thermal energy, or potential energy

Evaporation the process of a liquid turning into a gas at the surface of the liquid

Field a region around an object through which a force—for example, gravitational, electric, or magnetic—can be exerted

Force an influence that, if not counteracted, would produce a change in motion of an object

Friction resistance caused when one body is moved while in contact with another

Fundamental charge the smallest amount of electric charge, equivalent to the value of the charge on a proton or electron

Galaxy a group of stars that orbits a common center

Gravitational potential energy energy associated with the position of an object in a gravitational field

Gravity the attractive force between objects with mass

Hadron a group of fundamental particles that can experience the strong nuclear force

Infrared light with wavelengths longer than visible light

Insulator a material that does not allow the flow of electric current or thermal energy

Joule a unit of measurement for energy

Kinetic energy the energy an object has because of its motion

Large Hadron Collider a particle accelerator at CERN

Light-year the distance light travels in one year

Magnetic Resonance Imaging (MRI) a medical instrument that produces three-dimensional information about an object

Matter Anything that has mass and occupies space. All physical objects are made up of matter, and matter is made up of atoms.

Molecule the simplest structural unit of an element or chemical compound

Neutrino a fundamental particle with a very small mass and no electric charge

Neutron a hadron with a mass similar to a proton but with no electric charge

Newton a unit of measurement of force, equal to 0.22 pounds

Northern lights glowing patches of light sometimes visible in the night sky in the far northern latitudes

Nuclear reaction a reaction that changes an atom to another element

Nucleus the core of an atom where the protons and neutrons are

Oscillation motion back and forth in a repeating manner

Plasma Fourth and most common state of matter in the universe, distinct from solid, gaseous, or liquid matter

Polarization in an electrical sense, the separation of charges in a neutral object so that it interacts with other electrical charges

Positron aka positive electron; a positively charged subatomic particle that has the same mass and magnitude as the electron

Pressure a force divided by the area over which it is applied

Projectile motion the motion of an object that is under the influence of only the gravitational force

Proton a hadron with a fundamental positive electrical charge

Redshift the apparent shift in color toward longer wavelengths of an object moving away from an observer at a very high speed

Relativity the idea that fundamental physics depends on the motion of the observer

Solar wind the flow of charged particles that come from the sun

Standard Model the fundamental particles and interactions that govern the interactions of known matter

Standing wave a reflecting wave that interferes with itself

Static electricity the situation where electric charges on an object are stationary

Strong nuclear force an attractive interaction between hadrons

Superconductor a material that allows electric current to flow with no resistance at low temperatures

Super-Kamiokande a neutrino detector in Japan

Temperature a measure of the average kinetic energy of particles in an object

Terminal velocity the maximum velocity an object reaches while falling with air resistance

Thermal energy a form of energy transferred from one object to another in the form of heat

Thermal expansion an increase in size of an object as it increases in temperature

Trajectory the path of an object in motion

Vector a variable that has more than one dimension. Vectors usually have two or three dimensions.

Velocity the change in position divided by the change in time for an object in motion

Wavelength for a periodic wave, the distance from one wave crest to the next

About the Author

Rhett Allain spent most of his younger years in Illinois. In his youth, he enjoyed building things and taking things apart—although he couldn't always put them back together. He studied physics at the University of Alabama and North Carolina State University.

Currently, he is a blogger at Wired Science Blogs and a professor of physics. He lives with his wife and children in Louisiana, where he likes to ride his bike to work.

Acknowledgments

We would like to extend our thanks to the terrific team who worked so hard to make this project come together so quickly and so well.

Rovio

Sanna Lukander, Pekka Laine, Jan Schulte-Tigges, Mari Elomäki, and Anna Makkonen

National Geographic

Bridget A. English, Jonathan Halling, Susan Blair, Dan Sipple, Galen Young, Judith Klein, Anna Zusman, Lisa A. Walker, Anne Smyth, and Andrea Wollitz

CERN

Rolf Landua

Illustration Credits

Cover, OHiShiapply/Shutterstock; Back Cover, mexrix/Shutterstock; 4 (black and yellow border), Roobcio/Shutterstock; 5 (graph paper background), naihei/Shutterstock; 6 (wall and door), Peshkova/Shutterstock; 6 (background through door), Zurijeta/Shutterstock; 8-9, www.wendysmithaerial.com; 14-15, EvrenKalinbacak/Shutterstock.com; 17 (baseball player), Aspen Photo/Shutterstock.com; 17 (baseball), Alex Staroseltsev/Shutterstock; 18-19, TIMOTHY A. CLARY/AFP/Getty Images; 21 (woman), AlenD/Shutterstock; 21 (glass), kubais/Shutterstock; 22 (fire background), oldmonk/Shutterstock; 23 (black chalkboard on wooden wall), Tischenko Irina/Shutterstock; 23 (inset frame), IhorZigor/Shutterstock; 23 (inset Isaac Newton photo), Bettmann/Corbis; 25, Joggie Botma/Shutterstock; 27, marcovarro/Shutterstock; 29 (background), Mark Smith/Shutterstock; 29 (rocket), Lightspring/Shutterstock; 29 (woman), HomeArt/Shutterstock; 29 (woman's hair), Wally Stemberger/Shutterstock; 30 (blue background), Henry Hazboun/Shutterstock; 31 (black chalkboard on wooden wall), Tischenko Irina/Shutterstock; 31 (inset frame), LiliGraphie/Shutterstock; 31 (inset Galileo Galilei photo), Georgios Kollidas/Shutterstock; 33, NASA; 34-35, Racheal Grazias/Shutterstock; 35 (green car), Kolopach/Shutterstock; 37, Olga Bogatyrenko/Shutterstock; 38-39, Maxell Corporation of America/Manhattan Marketing Ensemble; 40 (coiled springs), based on Valdis Torms/Shutterstock; 42 (tuning fork), based on bayberry/Shutterstock; 43 (plants), based on Anthonycz/Shutterstock; 45, Dmitry Berkut/Shutterstock.com; 46-47, AP Photo/The Canadian Press, Jim Bradford; 48, Apatsara/Shutterstock; 51 (black chalkboard on wooden wall), Tischenko Irina/Shutterstock; 51 (inset frame), prosotphoto/Shutterstock; 51 (inset Chuck Yeager photo), U.S. Air Force/The U.S. National Archives and Records Administration, 542345; 52, Flip Nicklin/Minden Pictures/National Geographic Stock; 54-55, Imagemore Co., Ltd./Corbis; 59, Ted Kinsman/Science Source; 60 (canvas background), Fancy Studio/Shutterstock; 61 (black chalkboard on wooden wall), Tischenko Irina/Shutterstock; 61 (inset frame), Baloncici/iStockphoto; 61 (inset Alhazen photo), Wollertz/Shutterstock; 62, Mopic/Shutterstock; 64-65, Rutuparna Rayate/National Geographic My Shot; 67, Winfried Wisniewski/Foto Natura/National Geographic Stock; 68-69 (main hot air balloon image), Jill Fromer/iStockphoto.com; 69 (Red Angry Bird balloon), Based on Brandon Bourdages/Shutterstock.com; 70 (atom), based on AnastasiaSonne/Shutterstock; 72 (thermometer), based on gravitybox/iStockphoto; 74, Gunnar Pippel/Shutterstock; 77, Borge Ousland/National Geographic Stock; 78, Steven Bullen (www.raymears.com); 81, Mark Thiessen, NGS; 82 (background), based on original work/Shutterstock; 83 (black chalkboard on wooden wall), Tischenko Irina/Shutterstock; 83 (inset frame), Roobcio/Shutterstock; 83 (inset Alfred Nobel photo), www.imagebank.sweden.se, Gösta Florman/The Royal Library; 84-85 (plasma ball), Steve Allen/Brand X Pictures/Getty Images; 84-85 (background), STILLFX/Shutterstock; 87 (melting ice cream), Picsfive/Shutterstock; 87 (sidewalk background), Vincent Dale/iStockphoto; 88, Bob Thomas/iStockphoto; 91, Bruce & Greg Dale/National Geographic Stock; 92 (blue background), argus/Shutterstock; 93 (black chalkboard on wooden wall), Tischenko Irina/Shutterstock; 93 (inset frame), Maly Designer/Shutterstock; 93 (inset Nicolas Carnot photo), Photo Researchers/Colorization by Jessica Wilson; 94-95, Frans Lanting/National Geographic Stock; 97, Lawrence Manning/Corbis; 98-99, subtik/iStockphoto; 100 (Earth as magnet), based on Snowbelle/Shutterstock; 102 (lightbulb), based on Stock Elements/Shutterstock; 102 (battery), based on beboy/Shutterstock; 103 (magnet), based on unkreativ/Shutterstock; 104, Roger Ressmeyer/Corbis; 107, Beneda Miroslav/Shutterstock; 109 (black chalkboard on wooden wall), Tischenko Irina/Shutterstock; 109 (inset frame), Ortodox/Shutterstock; 109 (inset Michael Faraday photo), Georgios Kollidas/Shutterstock; 111, Ethan Daniels/Shutterstock; 112 (main image), BanksPhotos/iStockphoto; 112 (pole birds are sitting on), based on Kamenetskiy Konstantin/Shutterstock; 115 (main photo), Dave Reede/All Canada Photos/Corbis; 115 (sign), irin-k/Shutterstock; 116, Nata-Lia/Shutterstock; 118-119, Lijuan Guo/Shutterstock; 120 (background), Eliks/Shutterstock; 121 (black chalkboard on wooden wall), Tischenko Irina/Shutterstock; 121 (inset frame), Bennyartist/Shutterstock; 121 (inset Kristian Birkeland photo), Mondadori via Getty Images; 121 (inset solar flare), NASA/SDO/AIA; 121 (inset tape on paper), Picsfive/Shutterstock; 122, Nikada/iStockphoto.com; 124, granat/Shutterstock; 126-127, Teresa Levite/Shutterstock; 128-129 (Andromeda galaxy), Adam Evans/sky-candy.ca; 128 (rocket ship), voyager624/Shutterstock; 130 (Einstein), based on Bettmann/Corbis; 130 (feather), based on Potapov Alexander/Shutterstock; 134, The Milky Way galaxy as conceptualized by Ken Eward and National Geographic Maps; 137, NASA/WMAP Science Team; 138, NASA/ESA/National Geographic Image Collection; 141, Source: CERN; 142, NASA/Dana Berry; 144 ("Open" sign with brick wall background), antoniomas/Shutterstock; 144 (toucan), Valerie Loiseleux/iStockphoto; 144 (Café sign), based on Chad Littlejohn/Shutterstock; 147, Owaki/Kulla/Corbis; 148, Source: CERN; 151, NASA, ESA and R. Massey (California Institute of Technology); 152, Photo of The Super-Kamiokande Detector, The Institute for Cosmic Ray Research of the University of Tokyo; 154-155 (main image), Rebecca Pitt, for the exhibit "Discovering Particles: Fundamental Building Blocks of the Universe" (University of Birmingham and University of Cambridge); 154-155 (cloudy sky background), pio3/Shutterstock.

Bugs, Bugs, Bugs!

Butterflies

by Fran Howard

Consulting Editor: Gail Saunders-Smith, PhD

Consultant: Gary A. Dunn, MS, Director of Education
Young Entomologists' Society Inc.
Lansing, Michigan

Mankato, Minnesota

Pebble Plus is published by Capstone Press,
151 Good Counsel Drive, P.O. Box 669, Mankato, Minnesota 56002.
www.capstonepress.com

Printed in the United States of America

1 2 3 4 5 6 10 09 08 07 06 05

Library of Congress Cataloging-in-Publication Data
Howard, Fran, 1953–
Butterflies / by Fran Howard.
p. cm.—(Pebble plus: bugs, bugs, bugs!)
Includes bibliographical references and index.
ISBN-13: 978-0-7368-3643-2 (hardcover)
ISBN-10: 0-7368-3643-8 (hardcover)
ISBN-13: 978-0-7368-5101-5 (softcover pbk.)
ISBN-10: 0-7368-5101-1 (softcover pbk.)
1. Butterflies—Juvenile literature. I. Title. II. Series.
QL544.2.H69 2005
595.78'9—dc22 2004011970

Summary: Simple text and photographs describe the physical characteristics of butterflies.

Editorial Credits
Sarah L. Schuette, editor; Linda Clavel, set designer; Kate Opseth, book designer; Kelly Garvin, photo researcher; Scott Thoms, photo editor

Photo Credits
Bill Johnson, 14–15, 21
Brand X Pictures/Burke/Triolo, back cover
Bruce Coleman Inc./Gail M. Shumway, 6–7, 9; John Henry Williams, cover
Creatas, 1
Minden Pictures/Michael & Patricia Fogden, 5
Pete Carmichael, 17
Robert McCaw, 10–11
Sally McCrae-Kuyper, 13, 18–19

Note to Parents and Teachers

The Bugs, Bugs, Bugs! set supports national science standards related to the diversity of life and heredity. This book describes and illustrates butterflies. The images support early readers in understanding the text. The repetition of words and phrases helps early readers learn new words. This book also introduces early readers to subject-specific vocabulary words, which are defined in the Glossary section. Early readers may need assistance to read some words and to use the Table of Contents, Glossary, Read More, Internet Sites, and Index sections of the book.

Table of Contents

What Are Butterflies?

Butterflies are insects
with thin bodies
and large wings.

How Butterflies Look

Butterflies have
four colorful wings.

Most butterflies are about the size of a child's fist.

Butterflies have two antennas.
Butterflies use their antennas
to feel and smell.

Butterflies have thin legs.
Butterflies taste with
their feet.

What Butterflies Do

Butterflies drink nectar
from flowers.
Butterflies have long mouths
that work like straws.

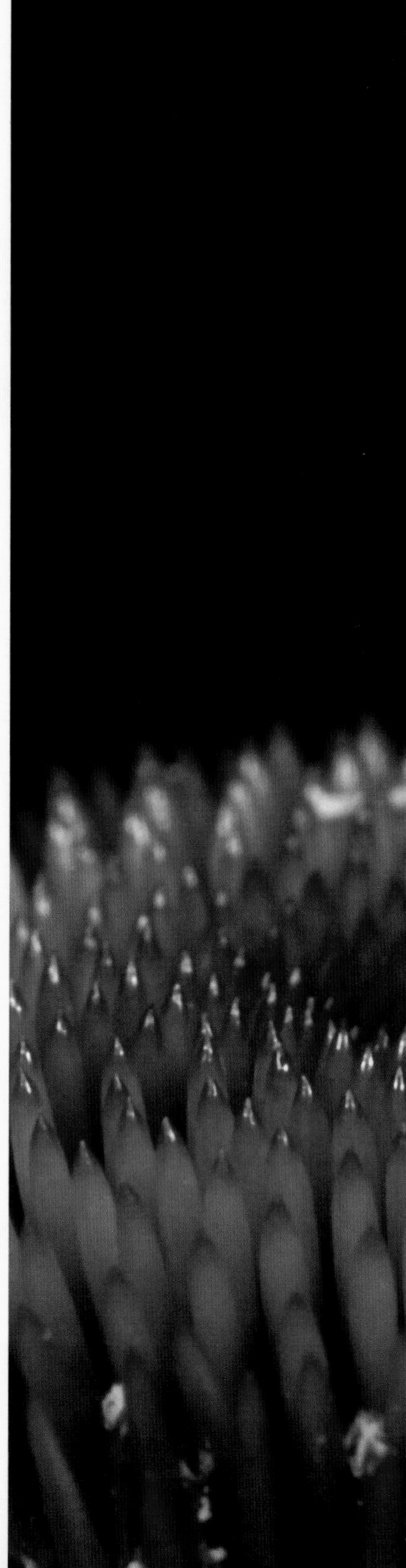

Butterflies fly from flower to flower. Pollen from the flowers sometimes sticks to their legs.

The pollen falls off when butterflies land on new flowers.

The pollen helps
new flowers grow.
More butterflies bring
more flowers.

Index

Word Count: 94
Grade: 1
Early-Intervention Level: 10